WORLD TALES

WORLD TALES

*The extraordinary coincidence of stories
told in all times, in all places*

The ISF Collectors' Library

Tales of A Parrot and Other Stories

The Happiest Man in The World
and Other Stories

The Food of Paradise
and Other Stories

The Water of Life and Other Stories

The Land Where Time Stood Still
and Other Stories

The Food of Paradise and Other Stories

VOLUME III

Collected by
IDRIES SHAH

The ISF Collectors' Library

'That lurking air of hidden meanings and immemorial mythical signs which we find in some fables, recalling a people, wise and childish at once, who had built up a theory of the world ages before Aesop was born.'
— Ernest Rhys, 1925

'The content of folklore is metaphysics. Our inability to see this is due primarily to our abysmal ignorance of metaphysics and its technical terms.'
— A. K. Coomaraswamy

'The folktale is the primer of the picture-language of the soul.'
— Joseph Campbell

'They (tales) appeal to our rational and irrational instincts, to our visions and dreams… The race is richer in human and cultural values for its splendid heritage of old magic tales.'
— Dr Leonard W. Roberts

Introduction

IT IS QUITE usual to find collections of tales arranged according to language or country: *Tales of Belgium*, *Stories from the German*, or *Legends from the Indian Peoples*; some such titles must have met your eye at one time or another. It all looks very tidy, scientific even; and the study of stories is indeed a part of scholarly research.

But the deeper you go into things, the more mysterious, exciting, baffling they become. How can it be that the same story is found in Scotland and also in pre-Columbian America? Was the story of Aladdin and his Wonderful Lamp really taken from Wales (where it has been found) to the ancient East; and, if so, by whom and when? A classical Japanese narrative is part of the gypsy repertoire in Europe; where shall we pigeonhole it in national terms?

I have selected and place before you a collection of tales of which one at least goes back to the ancient Egyptian of several thousand years ago. It is presented here not to impress the reader with its age, but because it is entertaining, and also because, although the Pharaohs died out many centuries ago, this tale is recited by people all over the world who know nothing of its origins. This form of culture remains when nations, languages and faiths have long since died.

There is an almost uncanny persistence and

durability in the tale which cannot be accounted for in the present state of knowledge. Not only does it constantly appear in different incarnations which can be mapped – as the Tar-Baby story carried from Africa to America, and medieval Arabian stories from the Saracens in Sicily to the Italy of today – but from time to time remarkable collections are assembled and enjoy a phenomenal vogue: after which they lapse and are reborn, perhaps in another culture, perhaps centuries later: to delight, attract, thrill, captivate yet another audience.

Such was the great *Panchatantra*, the Far Eastern collection of tales for the education of Indian princes; the Jataka Buddhist birth-stories believed to date back two and a half thousand years; the *Thousand and One Nights*, known as 'The Mother of Tales'. Later came the collections of Straparola, Boccaccio, Chaucer and Shakespeare, and a dozen others which now form the very basis of the classical literature of Europe and Asia.

This book contains stories from all of these collections, and many more: because there is a certain basic fund of human fictions which recur, again and again, and never seem to lose their compelling attraction. Many traditional tales have a surface meaning (perhaps just a socially uplifting one) and a secondary, inner significance, which is rarely glimpsed consciously, but which nevertheless acts powerfully upon our minds. Tales have always been used, so far as we can judge, for spiritual as well as social purposes: and as parables with more or less obvious meanings this use is familiar to most people today. But, as Professor Geoffrey Parrinder says of the myth, 'its inner truth was realised when the participant was transported into the realm of the sacred and eternal.'*

Perhaps above all the tale fulfils the function not of escape but of hope. The suspending of ordinary constraints helps people to reclaim optimism and to fuel the imagination with energy for the attainment of goals: whether moral or material. Maxim Gorky realised this when he wrote: 'In tales people fly through the air on a magic carpet, walk in seven-league boots, build castles overnight; the tales opened up for me a new world where some free and all-fearless power reigned and inspired in me a dream of a better life.'

When relatively recent collectors of tales, such as Hans Christian Andersen, the Brothers Grimm, Perrault and others made their selections, they both re-established certain powerful tales in our cultures and left out others from the very vast riches of the world reservoir of stories. Paradoxically, by their very success in imprinting Cinderella, Puss-in-Boots and Beauty and the Beast anew for the modern reader (they are all very ancient tales, widely dispersed) they directed attention away from some of the most wonderful and arresting stories which did not feature

---

* G. Parrinder, Foreword to *Pears Encyclopaedia of Myths and Legends*, London 1976, p.10.

in their collections. Many of these stories are re-presented here.

Working for thirty-five years among the written and oral sources of our world heritage in tales, one feels a truly living element in them which is startlingly evident when one isolates the 'basic' stories: the ones which tend to have travelled farthest, to have featured in the largest number of classical collections, to have inspired great writers of the past and present.

One becomes aware, by this contact with the fund of tradition which constantly cries out to be projected anew, that the story in some elusive way is the basic form and inspiration. Thought or style, characterisation and belief, didactic and nationality, all recede to give place to the tale which feels almost as if it is demanding to be reborn through one's efforts. And yet those efforts themselves, in some strange way, are experienced as no more than the relatively poor expertise of the humblest midwife. It is the tale itself, when it emerges, which is king.

Erskine Caldwell, no less, has felt a similar power in the story, and is well aware of its primacy over mere thought of philosophy: 'A writer,' he says (*Atlantic Monthly*, July 1958) 'is not a great mind, he's not a great thinker, he's not a great philosopher, he's a story-teller.'

Idries Shah

Note: This is the full introduction as it appeared in the original version of *World Tales*

Contents

Introduction   x

The Brahmin's Wife and the Mongoose: *India*   1

The Magic Bag: *Morocco*   5

Catherine's Fate: *Sicily*   10

The Desolate Island: *Palestine*   21

Gazelle Horn: *Tibet*   27

Tom Tit Tot: *England*   34

The Silent Couple: *Arabia*   43

Childe Rowland: *Scotland*   47

The Tale of Mushkil Gusha: *Persia*   57

The Food of Paradise: *Central Asia*   70

The Lamb with the Golden Fleece: *Europe*   87

The Man with the Wen: *Japan*   93

The Skilful Brothers: *Albania*   103

The Algonquin Cinderella: *North American Indian*   108

The Brahmin's Wife
and the Mongoose

This story must be one of the most popular in history. It is found in a Chinese collection dated to 412 AD, reputed to originate from the era of the great Indian emperor Ashoka –about 230 BC. It is still alive in the story-teller's repertoire in India, and was for centuries a favourite tale in Europe. It is found in the Greek translation of the Eastern Book of Sindibad, *and also in Latin, almost a hundred years before it was claimed to be an historical incident in the life of the Welsh Prince Llewellyn and his faithful hound Gellert, a greyhound presented to him in 1205 AD. There is, indeed, a Welsh proverb: 'I am as sorry as the man who killed his greyhound'. In some versions the mongoose becomes a wolf, or a snake, or even an eagle. In France, where the event was also believed to have occurred as an historical fact, the dog was, in*

the Middle Ages, regarded as a miracle-working martyr, and sick children were taken to his reputed grave. In Persian it is related as a Chinese tale; and it is also extant in Hebrew, Spanish and Syriac versions.

In India there flows a most holy river called the Ganges (named for the Goddess Ganga, Hindu divinity of the rivers), near the ancient city of Banaras. Near this city was a town called Mithila, where there dwelt a poor man, of the Brahmin faith and tradition, called Vidyadhara. He had no children, and he and his wife greatly loved, instead of a son or daughter, a tame mongoose.

For a long time the god Visvesvara and his wife Visalakshi observed this kindly pair, and so by divine power they blessed them with a son.

The child and the mongoose were brought up together, as twin brothers in the same cradle, for the Brahmin believed that the gods had given them a child because of their good behaviour towards the animal.

One day, in the morning, when the Brahmin had gone out to beg alms of the pious and charitable, and his wife was busy over her herb-pots, a snake glided through a hole in the garden wall.

The mongoose kept watch beside its young master, as usual, and saw its ancient enemy. The snake came towards the cradle, and hissed, fixing its glittering eyes upon the child.

Without a moment's hesitation, the brave little animal attacked the snake, and a fierce fight ensued. Soon the venomous cobra was dead, torn to pieces by the faithful mongoose.

Covered with blood, the mongoose ran to the child's mother with great excitement to show her what had been done.

'Oh, wretched mongoose!' cried she, following it to the room where the upturned cradle and blood-stained bedcovering showed no sign of the child. 'You have in your dreadful jealousy killed my son, the light of my eyes!' and with several strokes of the knife in her hand, she killed the creature.

But, crawling from a darkened corner of the room, the child laughed for joy, and the unhappy mother saw the mangled portions of the snake beside the cradle.

The mongoose had paid for the kindness which the Brahmin and his wife had shown it with its life.

The Magic Bag

This tale, told by a Berber tribesman in Morocco, has been said to date from the time when Christian priests and monks were still being challenged by local magicians who would not readily accept the new religion. North Africa certainly was Christianised before the Islamic conquest, and there is no way of telling whether this is the reason. On the other hand, the tale appears in similar form, with some of the same elements, both in Germany ('Brother Lustig') and in Italy ('Brother Giovannone') in which the hero is a monk and the bag is a gift from St Peter, who is eventually blackmailed into letting him into Paradise with the threat of its use. In the Sicilian version the monk actually imprisons Death in the bag, preventing people from dying as in the tale 'Occasion', in Book V *of this collection.*

There is a similarity, though not an identity, of this kind of tale with Central Asian ones where people with unusual powers are able to combat the normal reward-and-punishment routine laid down by local religion. Some versions, as in the case of a version from Tuscany, have the hero suspending his own demise (through trapping Death); he is hence called Godfather Misery, because 'Misery never ends'. In the telling of the same tale from Venice, where he is called Beppo Pipetta, he gets into Heaven by a trick. Refused admittance, he throws his cap in and then slips in and sits on it 'because I am sitting on my own property, and on my own property I do not take anyone's orders!'

THERE WAS ONCE a priest and a magician. The Priest said, 'It is only through me that you will get to Heaven.'

The Magician said, 'Is there no other way to achieve seemingly impossible things?'

'No,' said the Priest. 'We priests have the monopoly apart from some saints, but they are few and far between. As you know, they are almost all in the distant past.'

Now the Magician had a magical bag, and it could swallow anything its owner wanted. The Priest did not know that, but he was new in those parts, so that explained his confident manner.

The Magician said, 'If you have all the power, then you will not mind if I say to this bag, "Swallow the Priest!"'

'Not at all,' said the Priest, 'though it is a proof of your barbarian state, may your soul be saved!'

The Magician took up his bag and said to it, 'Swallow the Priest!'

The bag drew the Priest into itself, and he was never seen again.

Now the Magician decided that there was no need to allow priests, and others for that matter, to have all the dealings with the invisible world. So he always put into the bag any priests or monks who would not accept his claim to equal rights of intervention in matters such as these. In the end, most of the priests concentrated on exhorting people to do good, while the Magician used his bag to swallow people and things which were bad.

Finally a whole swarm of devils, voraciously hungry, because so much bad was disappearing without trace, tracked down the Magician. He told the bag to swallow them, and it did. But they were too tough for it to digest; the time for the total dissolution of demons had not yet arrived. So the Magician took the bag to a blacksmith. 'How much to hammer this bag completely flat, as slim as a knife-blade?' The smith said that he would do it for ten silver pieces. So he hammered day and night, but he could not get the bag flat. The demons, as is their habit, could always inflate themselves slightly after a blow had made them flat for a moment or two.

'You must have the devil in this bag!' shouted the furious and baffled smith. 'Yes, indeed I have,' said the Magician. Giving the smith only one silver piece for his trouble, he opened the bag and all the devils streamed out, back to Hell, feeling very battered.

Now the Magician carried on his life in much the same way, avoiding anything unpleasant by making it go into the magical bag, until it was nearly his time to die.

He went to see a wise Hermit about it. The Hermit said, 'If you have not been honed by pleasant and unpleasant things, you may get neither to Heaven nor to Hell, and you may cease to exist. But that is what some people want, anyway!'

When he died, the Magician found himself at the gates of Hell. 'Why am I here since I got rid of so much evil in my life?' he asked the demon at the gate. The demon looked in his book. 'Because you spent so much time concentrating on bad things that you have a natural affinity for us – come in,' he said.

The Magician did not like the sound of this at all, so he said to the bag, which was over his shoulder, 'Swallow all this!' In a twinkling of an eye there was no Hell to be seen.

The Magician made his way to Heaven. At the gate he was stopped. 'I have to come in!' he said.

'Why?' asked the angel on duty.

'Because Hell has ceased to exist, and there is no other place to go.'

'I can get Heaven into this bag in a twinkling of an eye, and you, too, if you don't let me in!'

And that, they say, is how he got into Heaven.

But there are some who say that the places he visited were not Heaven or Hell at all.

But you just decide, as I have given you all the help I can, and it is nearly time for me to jump into my magical bag.

Catherine's Fate

If it were to be asked 'What are world tales actually about?'
– the answer would have to be 'They are about fate or destiny.'
Some cover a long life, some only a few incidents from a career.
Some are supposed to be about the lives of real people, others
purport to cover happenings – which can still be called 'fate' –
in the lives of mythical creatures. Fairies and superstitions are
instruments of fate, too: the fairy godmother alters fate, and
the rabbit's-foot is carried in the hope that it will cause a
favourable fate.

 Fairy tales are often imagined to be so named because they
feature gentle feminine apparitions with gauzy wings. This is
only a recent idea. The word fairy comes from the Latin fata
(fate), which became 'enchantment' in French. So fate and
magic are always associated in traditional tales: and the kind
of 'fairy' found in modern Western story-books, usually for
children, is only one form of this concretised Fate.

 In this tale, found in Sicily and known in the Far East as
well, Catherine's Fate takes a more direct and positive form, as

an imposing woman.

In Greek and Roman times, there were believed to be three Fates, which arbitrarily controlled every person's life. Of these, Lachesis measured the Thread of Life; and the special thread which features in this story may indicate an improvement in life, and eventual happiness, bestowed by Lachesis.

THERE ONCE LIVED a very rich and generous merchant who had a gorgeous palace. The pride of his life was his daughter, a beautiful creature called Catherine. Catherine was tall and slim, with black hair and large, lustrous eyes. Her hands and feet were small and delicate, her skin as soft as the petals of a rose.

In the palace there were thrones of gold, chairs of silver set with precious turquoises, picture-frames set with rubies, water-jugs set with diamonds. All around her was luxury and beauty. Peacocks strolled in the gardens, flowers bloomed in pots hanging from the trees; all was the best that money could buy.

One day, when Catherine was walking in the garden, dressed in long silken robes sewn with the finest pearls and a cap with tassels of pearls, a very elegant-looking lady appeared before her.

There was an extraordinary look about this lady, her eyes were very penetrating and dark, her clothes did not seem to be anything but luminous draperies.

'Catherine, my dear child,' said the lady, 'what would you rather have: would you like to enjoy your life in your youth, or would you like to enjoy it in your old age? You have only these two choices.'

Catherine thought for a moment, and then she said: 'If I have my enjoyment now, will I suffer for it in my last years?'

And the tall lady said, 'Yes.'

'But how do you know?' asked Catherine, still

pondering the question.

'I am your Fate,' answered the apparition.

'Oh, then I will have my good fortune in my old age,' said Catherine.

'Very well, so be it,' said her Fate, and vanished.

Catherine thought nothing of this encounter, and returned to the house to change her clothes for something even finer. But a few days later, terrible things began to happen.

There was a great storm at sea. Catherine's father had expected his ships to return from a foreign country, loaded with rich cargoes, and they were all sent, by the tempest, to the bottom of the sea.

His warehouses were gutted by a mysterious fire, so when he decided to refit new ships, there was nothing to put in them. He hired his ships to a duke who wanted to go to war with another prince, and all the ships were sunk in an engagement with pirates. The duke's men were put to the sword, and he, too, was penniless.

Thieves broke in and stole all Catherine's jewels; her clothes had to be sold to keep them in food a little longer. At last, wretched and ill, Catherine's father died, leaving her alone in the world. Penniless and in very simple garments, Catherine decided to leave this unlucky city and find some work, if possible, in another place. So she said farewell to the city of her birth, and trudged off.

She eventually reached a noble city far from her own country, and was standing in the street, wondering which way to go. She only had a little money, given to her by an old nurse, and was wondering where she could buy a piece of bread.

A lady of quality, looking out of her window, saw her and called out: 'Who are you, my dear, and where do you come from? You are not from this part of the land.'

'Lady, I am all alone in the world, as my father, who was once a rich merchant, has died, and I am looking for somewhere to buy a piece of bread,' she said.

'Come into my house, I need a servant, and you will do very well,' said the noblewoman, and Catherine went gratefully inside the big house.

The lady became very fond of Catherine, and trusted her with all the things she possessed. One day the mistress said to her:

'I have to go out for a little while; lock the door behind me, and let no one either in or out until I return.'

So Catherine locked the door, and sat down by the fire. No sooner had the noblewoman gone, than the door flew open and her Fate entered.

'So, here you are, Catherine!' cried her Fate harshly. 'You have found yourself a very nice place here, haven't you? Well, you can't escape me like that you know!' and she began to throw the mistress's valuables all over the floor, breaking glass and china, and tearing priceless linen to pieces.

'Oh, no, no, no,' cried Catherine, 'I shall get into the most dreadful trouble! The lady trusts me!'

'Oh, does she?' sneered her Fate. 'Well, explain this to her when she comes back then!' and she ripped the long silken curtains to tatters.

Catherine put her hands to her face and ran from the house, never looking back in case her Fate was following.

No sooner had she gone, than her Fate put everything back exactly as it had been before, and disappeared.

When the lady came back the house was perfectly tidy, but Catherine was gone. The mistress called and called, but of course the poor girl did not hear, for she was far away.

The lady looked everywhere, and thought perhaps Catherine had robbed her, but nothing was missing. She could not understand what could have happened, the girl had seemed to be perfectly reliable.

Now poor Catherine ran on until she reached another city, and when looking for somewhere to buy a piece of bread, was noticed by another lady standing at her window.

The lady opened the window and said to her: 'Where are you from, and what are you doing in this place, when so obviously you seem to be lost?'

'I am a poor girl from far away, and I am looking for something to eat, as I am very hungry,' said Catherine.

'Well, come into my house,' said the lady, 'I will feed you and clothe you, and you may have a position in my household.'

So Catherine went in. But the very same thing happened as before. No sooner was she settled in the house, and trusted with all the valuables, than her Fate appeared, and created chaos in a few seconds.

'Do you think that there was anywhere in this world I would not be able to find you?' cried her Fate harshly, sweeping a line of priceless scent-bottles to the ground and smashing them to smithereens. Catherine put her hands to her face and ran.

And so it went on for the space of seven years. Each time Catherine was taken on by some nice lady, the appearance of her Fate caused her to travel on and on, endlessly, it seemed to her. But she never escaped for long.

But, and this Catherine did not know, her Fate always restored everything to its former state the minute Catherine had disappeared.

Now seven years passed in this manner, and when Catherine was working for a very noble lady with a very kind heart, it was almost as if Catherine's Fate had forgotten about her. Day after day, Catherine looked after the house, and things were always right for her. The tension was very great, though, for every hour she expected the door to fly open and her Fate to appear.

Each day, she had to go up the mountain with a basket of the finest bread and cheese for her mistress. A tall, dignified personage took the bread from her gracefully each day, and after bowing, disappeared into a cave.

One day her mistress told her: 'I always have to propitiate my Fate in this way. If that fresh bread and cheese were not sent to her, I shudder to think what she might cause to happen to me.'

At this Catherine began to weep, unable to hide her grief, for she had suffered so much in the last seven years that she could no longer hide her sadness.

'My dear child, what is the matter with you? Tell me at once!' cried the kind-hearted mistress, placing her hand on Catherine's shoulder.

So Catherine told her the story of her Fate's cruelty, and continued, 'I do not think that I can stand any more of this anguish, expecting her to appear any moment and to tear everything to pieces, as she has done so often. In fact, I would like to go away from here, soon, so that I do not bring my Fate's destruction upon this house.'

'Now, let me think of a plan,' said the noble-woman, striking her forehead. 'Yes, I have it. When you go up the mountain with my Fate's bread, tell her your story, and appeal to her to have a word with your Fate, that she leaves off tormenting you like this. I am sure my Fate, who is kind, will help.'

So, next day, when Catherine went up to the mountain with the bread for her mistress's Fate, she asked her to intercede with her own Fate. 'Well, your Fate is asleep under seven quilts, just now,' said the lady's Fate, 'but when you come tomorrow she might be awake and I will take you to her.'

Catherine went away full of hope, and slept that night quite peacefully.

When she took the bread up the mountain next morning, her mistress's Fate took her to her own Fate, who lay in a large bed, covered to the eyes with seven feather quilts.

'Now sister, here is Catherine,' said the Fate of the noblewoman. 'Leave off tormenting her so; I beg you to give her a little rest now.'

Her Fate said nothing but, 'Here is a skein of silk, look after it carefully, it will be of great use to you, now leave me to rest.' And she pulled the quilts over her head.

Puzzled by this, Catherine went home. Her mistress was all agog to know what had happened, but could not make head nor tail of the story Catherine told her. 'The silk is worth scarcely anything,' she said, 'but you had better keep it. It might be of some use, as your Fate said.'

The King of that country, who was young and extremely handsome, was to marry, and there was much consternation at the royal tailor's, when it was discovered that no silk of the right colour to sew the King's wedding robe together was to be found in the entire kingdom.

'Issue a proclamation,' said the King, 'I must have my robes done in time! Send to the four countries bordering my land, send to every quarter of my dominions! Whoever has silk of this colour must bring it to the court, and I shall reward the owner of the silk generously.'

The noblewoman heard the proclamation and came to tell Catherine, 'Catherine, my child, put on this dress and take your skein to the court. It is exactly the colour the King's tailor is looking for,' she cried excitedly. 'You will be rewarded most generously, I am sure.'

When Catherine appeared at the Court before the throne, the young King found her so beautiful to look upon that he could not take his eyes off her face.

'Your Majesty,' said she, 'will this silk be suitable for your wedding robe?'

'You shall be paid in pure gold for it,' said the King. 'Bring the scales, and we will weigh the skein; whatever it weighs, you shall have the equivalent in the finest gold of my realm.'

They brought the scales, but no matter how much gold was put upon the scales, the skein was always heavier.

Then the King had larger scales brought, and threw all his treasure on to the scales, and still the skein weighed more.

Then, in extreme exasperation, the King took the crown from his head and put it on the scales. At that very second the scales balanced and the King laughed.

'Where did you get this silk, my dear?' he asked Catherine.

'From my mistress,' said Catherine, and the King shouted, 'Impossible! What sort of lady is your mistress that she has magic silk like this?'

Then Catherine told all that had happened to her to the King, and he took her hand in his. 'I will marry you instead of the girl to whom I have been betrothed,' he said, and so it happened.

Afterwards, Catherine, who had suffered so much in her youth, lived to be a very old woman, and was happy until the moment of her death as Queen of that far country.

The Desolate Island

About the first half of the seventh century was written a spiritual romance, supposedly about Barlaam and Josaphat, by a monk named John of Damascus. It was not until many centuries later that it was realised that most of the material in this book related to the life of the Buddha, and not to any Christian saint. The tenth parable in the work is also found in the Talmud, and employed there to encourage good and thoughtful deeds. Its substance was widely used by medieval monks to warn their hearers to prepare for the world to come, and it is also found in the oldest Spanish storybook, Count Lucanor, *of the 14th century. This is the Talmudic Parable of the* Desolate Island, *where the rich man is God, the slave is man, the island the world, the year of reign his lifespan, and the desolate island the future world.*

Scholars are of the opinion that the myth based on the Buddhist sources (which are still extant) was composed in pre-Islamic Egypt. There is also a literary and oral legend that the Caliph Haroun Al Rashid carried out an experiment, placing a stranger, after drugging him, on the throne to test his worth; then drugging him again and returning him to his former place, because of his abuse of power. In a Sufi parable, a master hypnotises a self-styled godly man, places him on a throne, reveals that he is really greedy, and restores him to his pauperhood, saying to the King and disciples (for whom the demonstration is performed): 'This is not our man.' The phrase has accordingly become a proverb in the Middle East.

THERE WAS ONCE a very wealthy man, who was of a kind and generous disposition, and who wanted to make his slave happy. He therefore gave him his freedom, and also presented him with a shipload of merchandise.

'Go,' he said, 'and sail to various countries. Dispose of these goods, and whatever you may get for them shall be your own.'

The freed slave sailed away, across the wide ocean.

He had not been long on his voyage before a storm blew up. His ship was driven on to the rocks and went to pieces, and all on board were lost except the former slave himself. He managed to swim to a nearby island and drag himself ashore.

Sad, despondent and lonely, naked and with nothing to his name, he walked across the land until he came to a large and beautiful city.

Many people came out to meet him, crying, 'Welcome! Welcome! Long live our King!'

They brought a rich carriage and, placing him in it, escorted him to a magnificent palace, where many servants gathered around him. He was dressed in royal garments and they addressed him as their sovereign: they expressed their complete obedience to his will.

The ex-slave was, naturally enough, amazed and confused, wondering whether he was dreaming; and all that he saw, heard or experienced was merely passing fantasy.

Eventually he became convinced that what was happening was in fact real; and he asked some people around him, whom he liked, how he could have arrived in this state.

'I am, after all,' he said, 'a man of whom you know nothing, a poor, naked wanderer, whom you have never seen before. How can you make me your ruler? This causes me more amazement than I can possibly say.'

'Sire,' they answered, 'this island is inhabited by spirits. Long ago they prayed that they might be sent a son of man to rule over them, and their prayers have been answered. Every year they are sent a son of man. They receive him with great dignity and place him on the throne. But his status and his power end when the year is over. Then they take the royal robes from him and put him on board a ship, which carries him to a vast and desolate island. Here, unless he has previously been wise and prepared for that day, he finds neither subject nor friend: and he is obliged to pass a weary, lonely and miserable life. Then a new King is selected, and so year follows year. The Kings who came before you were careless and did not think. They enjoyed their power to the full, forgetting the day when it would end.'

These people counselled the former slave to be wise, and to allow their words to stay within his heart.

The new King listened carefully to all this: and he felt grieved that he should have wasted even the little time which had passed since he came to the island.

He asked a man of knowledge who had already spoken:

'Advise me, O Spirit of Wisdom, how I may prepare for the days which will come upon me in the future.'

'Naked you came among us,' said the man, 'and naked you shall be sent to the desolate island of which I have told you. At present you are King, and may do whatever you please. Therefore, send workmen to the island, and let them build houses and prepare the land, and make the surroundings beautiful. The barren soil will be turned into fruitful fields, people will go there to live, and you will have established a new kingdom for yourself. Your own subjects will be waiting to welcome you when you arrive. The year is short, the work is long: therefore be earnest and energetic.'

The King followed this advice. He sent workmen and materials to the desolate island and, before the end of his term of power, it had become a fertile, pleasant and attractive place. The rulers who had come before him had anticipated the end of their time with fear, or smothered the thought of it by amusing themselves. But he looked forward to it with joy, for then he could start upon a career of permanent peace and happiness.

And the day came. The freed slave who had been made a king was stripped of his authority. With his royal robes he lost his powers. He was placed naked on a ship, and its sails were set for the island. When he approached its shore, however, the people whom he had sent ahead came forward to welcome him with music, song and great joy. They made him ruler, and he lived ever after in peace.

Gazelle Horn

The Hindu and Buddhist scriptures and tale collections contain many stories which are substantially similar to variants known all over the world. Among these ancient writings are the Hindu Mahabharata *and* Ramayana *and the Tibetan Buddhist* Kangyur *and* Tangyur, *which have influenced peoples of the Far East with tales which have not diffused westwards: 'Gazelle Horn' is one of the best-known examples of this.*

Some idea of the importance of these books is seen in the fact that one collection of the Kangyur *was bartered by a Buriat community for 7,000 oxen: even though, as the Russian authority Vasilev notes, people listen to the recitations and 'are edified, even though they do not comprehend' – since they do not understand Tibetan.*

The Kangyur *is a translation from Sanskrit sources, made in Tibet between the 7th and 13th centuries, but mostly in the 9th. Its contents were analysed by the Hungarian pioneering scholar Csoma Korosi in Calcutta from a hundred-volume edition. This version is, however, taken from the 108-volume edition printed in Peking in the 18th century by command of the Emperor, and translated by Professor Franz Anton Schiefner, the specialist in Buddhist legends.*

IN VERY REMOTE times, in a forest region free from villages and richly provided with flowers, fruits, water and roots, there lived a penance-performing holy man, a Rishi. He fed on roots, fruit and water, and clothed himself with leaves and skins.

As he had attained the Five Kinds of Insight, wild gazelles were in the habit of living in his hermitage, keeping him company. One day a gazelle doe came to the spot where he had lately been. And, as the results of human actions are beyond mental comprehension, it happened that she became pregnant. When the time came for her to bring forth, she went back to the same place and there gave birth to a boy.

When she had smelt him and realised that this was a creature that did not resemble herself, she was terrified, and abandoned him. Now the Rishi came to the place and saw the child. He began to consider whose it might be; and he perceived that it was his own child. So he took the baby with him into his hermitage and brought it up there. When the boy had grown, gazelle horns appeared on his head, and because of this the Rishi named him Gazelle Horn.

The Rishi fell ill, and although treated with the right medicines, his sickness did not become less. Seeing that he must die soon, he spoke to the boy thus:

'O son, from time to time many Rishis come to this hermitage from all manner of regions. You must, from love of me, receive them in a friendly manner, invite them to repose on the couch, and set before them roots and fruits according to your means.'

It is said that the end of collection is diffusion; the end of the high is to fall; the end of coming together is separation; and the end of life is death. So the holy man discharged his obligations to this law. The youth burnt the Rishi's body in the usual manner and then, as he mourned, being depressed by grief at the loss of his father, he found himself possessed of the Five Kinds of Insight.

One day, when he had gone to fetch water in a pitcher, the deity began to let rain fall. As he walked along with the container, which was quite full, he let it fall, so that it broke. Rishis are very quickly angered; so, spilling the little water that was left, he reproached the deity, saying: 'As my full pitcher has been broken because of your bad behaviour, you shall not let rain fall for twelve years from this day!'

Because of this curse, the deity let no rain fall. In consequence, a great famine arose in Varanasi and its people consequently emigrated in all directions.

The King sent for the seers and said to them: 'Honoured Sirs, to whose power is it due that the deity sends no rain?'

They replied, 'To a Rishi's anger. If he can be disturbed in his penances, the deity will again send rain. Otherwise it is not possible.'

The King sat, absorbed in thought. His wives, the

30

Princes and the Ministers asked him, 'Why, O King, are you displeased?'

He replied: 'On account of a Rishi's anger the deity sends no rain. The seers have declared that if the Rishi can be disturbed in his penances the deity will send rain again, but that otherwise it is impossible.'

One of the King's daughters, whose name was Shanta, said, 'O King, if that is the case, do not be distressed. I will contrive that the Rishi shall be completely distracted from this penance.'

The King said, 'By what means?'

She replied, 'Let me and other women be taught mystic lore by the Brahmins, members of the priestly caste. And let a hermitage, provided with flowers, fruit and water, be prepared on a ferry boat.' The King agreed.

Then the Princess gave orders for the preparation of tempting objects, and fruits filled with wine, and other very bright fruits of various kinds. She made herself look like a Rishi, dressed herself in bark and grass, and went to the Gazelle Horn Rishi's hermitage, attended by the women to whom the Brahmins had taught mystic lore.

When they arrived, the pupils of the Gazelle Horn Rishi said to him, 'O Teacher! Many Rishis have come to the Hermitage.'

He replied: 'It is well that Rishis have come. Bring them in.'

When they had entered and he had looked at them, he said in verse:

'Alas! A Rishi's appearance was never like this of old:

'A loosely flowing step, a face free from beard, a rising and falling breast.'

His mind was a prey to doubt, but he offered his visitors roots and fruit. They ate, and then said to the Rishi, 'Your fruits are harsh and acid. The fruits which are to be found at our hermitage on the water are like the drink of the gods. Therefore we invite you there.'

He went with them to the pleasure-ground on board the boat. There they spread before him stupefying substances, coconuts filled with wine, and other fruits. When he was drunk with wine and seduced by the alluring things, he gave himself up to pleasure with the women, and his magical power vanished.

The deity, rejoicing in rain, called the clouds together from every side and got the better of the Rishi.

Shanta said, 'Now, do you know what the power is?'

Having fettered the Rishi with amorous bonds, she took him to the King and said, 'O King! This is the man.'

As the deity now sent rain, a good harvest followed. The King gave Shanta to the Rishi as his wife, together with her attendants. But the Rishi, ignoring her, began to indulge in love with other women. She also started to treat him with small respect, as her good nature was destroyed by jealousy.

One day, when she hit him on the head with a shoe during an argument, he said to himself:

'I, who used not to allow power to the thunder of the cloud, must now, being fettered by love bonds, allow myself to be set at naught by a woman!'

Thereupon he again devoted himself to ascetic exertions, and once more became possessed of the Five Kinds of Insight.

Tom Tit Tot

The power resident in a person's name is a feature of folklore in widely dispersed cultures. It is very likely that this native English version of the imp and his secret name was current in the British Isles for many centuries before it was driven out by the Grimm Brothers' exportation of the German form – now better known in Anglo-Saxon countries – Rumpelstiltskin. The secret name, and the forfeit which has to be given if it cannot be discovered, is widely reflected in folktales. There is a cognate of Tom Tit Tot in southern Nigeria, 'The Hippopotamus called Isantim'. The tale is found in places as far apart as Iceland and Italy, Mongolia and Sweden. In Cornwall the secret name is Terrytop; in Scotland, Whuppity Stoorie, in France, Ricdin-Ricdon, and in Magyar, Dancing Vargaluska. This English version, taken down from the words of an East Anglian woman a century ago, is beautifully told – the folklorist Joseph Jacobs thought it 'far superior to any of the Continental variants'.

ONCE UPON A time there was a woman who had baked five pies. When they came from the oven, they had been so over-baked that their crusts were too hard to eat.

So the lady said to her daughter:

'Maiden, you just put those pies on the shelf and leave them there, and the pastry will get soft.'

But she didn't say, 'They'll get soft', really, she said, in the way they have in East Anglia, 'They'll come again', meaning the same thing.

But the girl, hearing these words, said to herself:

'Well, if they'll come again, I'll eat them now.' And she sat down and, there and then, ate them all up.

When it was time for supper, the woman said to the girl:

'Go and get one of those pies. I expect they've come again now.'

The girl went and she looked, and there was nothing there but the pie-dishes. So she went back to her mother, and she said:

'No, they haven't come again.'

'Not one of them?' asked the mother.

'Not one of them,' she said.

'Well, whether they've come again or not come again,' said the mother, 'I'll have one for my supper.'

'But you can't, if they haven't come,' said the girl.

'But I can,' said she, 'go and bring the best of them.'

'Best or worst,' said the girl, 'I've eaten them all,

and you can't have one until it has come again.'

Well, the woman was really angry, and she took her spinning to the door to spin, and as she spun she sang:

'My daughter has eaten five, five pies today –
My daughter has eaten five, five pies today.'

The King was coming down the street, and he heard her singing, but he could not make out the words. So he stopped, and he said:

'What was that you were singing about, Mother?'

The woman was ashamed to let him know what her daughter had done, so she sang, instead of that:

'My daughter has spun five, five skeins today,
My daughter has spun five, five skeins today.'

'Well!' said the King, 'I never heard of anyone who could do that.'

Then he said: 'Look here, I want a wife, and I'll marry your daughter. But take note: eleven months of the year she shall have all the food she likes to eat, and all the gowns she wants to wear, and all the company she cares to have. But, the last month of the year, she'll have to spin five skeins every day – and if she does not, I'll kill her!'

'All right,' said the woman, for she was thinking what a fine marriage that would be. And as for those five skeins, well, there would be plenty of ways of getting out of that – most likely he'd forget about it.

And so they were married. And for eleven months the girl had all the food she wished, and all the dresses she desired, and all the company she wanted. But, when the time was ending, she began to think about those skeins, and she wondered whether the King still had them in mind. But not one word did he say about them: and she thought that he must have forgotten the whole matter.

However, on the last day of the last month of the eleven, he took her into a room which she had never seen before. There was nothing in it but a spinning wheel and a stool.

'Now,' he said, 'now my dear, you will be shut in here tomorrow with some food and some flax. And, if you haven't spun five skeins by nightfall, your head will come off!'

And away he went, about his business.

Well, she was very frightened indeed. She had always been a useless girl, so much so that she did not even know how to spin. What was she to do tomorrow, with nobody to help her? She sat down on a stool in the kitchen, and how she cried!

Then she suddenly heard a hard kind of knocking on the door. She jumped up and opened it; and what did she see but a small black thing with a long tail, who looked at her strangely, and said:

'What are you a-crying for?'

'What's that to you?' she asked.

'Never you mind,' he said, 'but tell me what you're crying for.'

'It won't do me any good if I do,' said she.

'You don't know that,' said the visitor, and its tail twirled around.

'Well,' she said, 'it won't do any harm, even if it does no good,' and she told him all about the pies and the skeins and everything.

'This is what I'll do,' said the little black thing: 'I'll come to your window in the morning and take the flax – and bring it spun at night.'

'What would you charge?' she asked.

It looked out of the corner of its eye and said:

'I'll give you three chances every night to guess my name. And, if you haven't guessed it before the month is up, you shall be mine!'

Well, she thought, she'd be sure to guess the name before the month was up.

'All right,' said she, and how the thing twisted its tail with delight!

Well, the next day, her husband took her into the room, and there was the flax and the day's food.

'Now, there's the flax,' said he, 'and if you haven't spun it by night, off goes your head!'

And then he went out and locked the door.

He had hardly gone when there was a knocking on the window. She leapt up and opened it, and there – sure enough – was the little old thing sitting on the ledge.

'Where's the flax?' he said.

'Here it is,' she said. And she handed it over.

Well, when evening came, there was a rapping on the window again. She got up and opened it, and there was the little old thing, with five skeins of flax on his arm.

'Here it is,' he said, and he gave it to her.

'Now, what's my name?'

'Is it Bill?' she asked.

'No, it is not,' he said.

And he twirled his tail.

'Is it Ned?'

'No it is not.'

And he twirled his tail.

'Well, is it Mark?'

'No, it is not.' And he twirled his tail harder.

And away he flew.

Well, when her husband came in, there were the five skeins, ready for him.

'I see I shan't have to kill you tonight, my dear,' said he. 'You'll have your food and flax in the morning' – and away he went.

After that, the flax and food were brought, and every day the little black imp came, morning and evening. And all day the maiden was sitting thinking of names to say when he came at night.

But she never lit on the right one. And, as the days approached the end of the month, the imp began to look really malicious, and twirled his tail faster every time she made a guess.

At last it came to the last day but one. The imp came that night with the usual five skeins and said:

'What, haven't you got my name yet?'

'Is it Nicodemus?' she asked.

'No, it is not,' he said.

'Is it Samuel?' she wanted to know.

'No, it is not,' said he.

'Well, then is it Methuselah?'

'No, it is not that, either,' he said; and he looked at her like a fiery coal, and said:

'Woman, there's only tomorrow night – then you'll be mine!' And away he flew.

Well, she really did feel horrid. But then she heard the King coming along the corridor. In he came, and when he saw the five skeins, he said:

'Well, my dear, I can see that you'll have your skeins tomorrow night as well and – as I reckon I shan't have to kill you, I'll have supper in here tonight.'

So supper was brought, and another stool for him, and down the two sat to eat.

Well, the King had not had more than about a mouthful, when he stopped and began to laugh.

'What is it?' she asked.

'Because,' he said, 'I was out hunting today, and I got to a place in the wood which I hadn't seen before. And there was an old chalk pit, and a sort of humming sound. So I got off my horse and went very quietly to the pit, and I looked down.

'Well, what should be there, but the funniest little black thing you should ever see. And what was it doing, but spinning wonderfully fast with a little spinning-wheel and twirling its tail. And as it spun, it sang:

"'Nimmy nimmy not,
My name's Tom Tit Tot".'

Well, when the maiden heard this, she felt as if she could have jumped out of her skin for joy – but she didn't say a word.

Next day, the little thing looked really nasty when he came for the flax. And, when night fell, the girl heard that tapping again on the window-pane. She opened the window, and the imp came right in on the ledge. It was grinning from ear to ear, and how its tail was twirling!

'What's my name?' it asked, as it gave her the skeins.

'Is it Solomon?' she said, pretending to be afraid.

'No, it is not!' As he said that he came further into the room.

'Well, is it Zebedee?' she said.

'No, it is not!' And then it laughed and twirled its tail until you could hardly see it.

'Take time, woman!' it said, 'for there is one more guess and you're mine!' And it stretched out its black hands at her.

She backed away a step or two, and she looked

at it, and then she laughed out loud, and she said, pointing a finger at it:

'Nimmy nimmy not,
Your name's Tom Tit Tot.'

When he heard that, he gave an awful shriek, and flew into the dark, and she never saw him, ever again.

The Silent Couple

A famous Scottish ballad, 'The Barring of the Door', is essentially the same tale as that of the Silent Couple, which is one of the world's most widely distributed folktales. It is found in Turkey and Sri Lanka, in Venice and Kashmir, in Arabia and Sicily, and quite possibly in many other places as well. If it came from the East, its route to Scotland is mysterious. If it originates in the West, how it found itself in several distinct Asian cultures is no less intriguing. This is the Arabian version.

ONCE UPON A time there was a newly married couple; still dressed in their wedding finery, they relaxed in their new home when the last of the guests at their feast had left.

'Dear husband,' said the young lady, 'do go and close the door to the street, which has been left open.'

'Me shut it?' said the groom. 'A bridegroom in this splendid costume, with a priceless robe and a dagger studded with jewels? How could I be expected to do such a thing? You must be out of your mind. Go and shut it yourself.'

'So!' shouted the bride, 'you expect me to be your slave: a gentle, beautiful creature like me, wearing a dress of finest silk – that I should get up on my wedding day and close a door which looks onto the public street? Impossible.'

They were both silent for a moment or two, and the lady suggested that they should make the problem the subject of a forfeit. Whoever spoke first, they agreed, should be the one to shut the door.

There were two sofas in the room, and the pair settled themselves, face to face, one on each, sitting mutely looking at one another.

They had been in this posture for two or three hours when a party of thieves came by and noticed that the door was open. The robbers crept into the silent house, which seemed so deserted, and began to load themselves with every portable object of any

44

value which they could find.

The bridal couple heard them come in, but each thought that the other should attend to the matter. Neither of them spoke or moved as the burglars went from room to room, until at length they entered the sitting room and at first failed to notice the utterly motionless couple.

Still the pair sat there, while the thieves collected all the valuables, and even rolled up the carpets under them. Mistaking the idiot and his stubborn wife for wax dummies, they stripped them of their personal jewels – and still the couple said nothing at all.

The thieves made off, and the bride and her groom sat on their sofas throughout the night. Neither would give up.

When daylight came, a policeman on his beat saw the open street door and walked into the house. Going from room to room he finally came upon the pair and asked them what was happening. Neither man nor wife deigned to reply.

The policeman called massive reinforcements and the swarming custodians of the law became more and more enraged at the total silence, which to them seemed obviously a calculated affront.

The officer in charge at last lost his temper and called out to one of his men: 'Give that man a blow or two, and get some sense out of him!'

At this the wife could not restrain herself: 'Please,

kind officers,' she cried, 'do not strike him – he is my husband!'

'I won!' shouted the fool immediately, 'so you have to shut the door!'

Childe Rowland

How can an ancient Inca story have been current in Shakespeare's time as an English folktale, mentioned in King Lear? *A Guatemalan Indian provided the traditional materials for the* Popul Vuh, *for the Spanish conquerors, containing this story. It was described by Lewis Spence as 'the only native American work that has come down to us from pre-Columbian times'. It features a game with a ball, and the penetration of the underground headquarters of magically endowed people — who capture mortals by two young heirs to a gracious lady, for the purpose of a battle. An adviser warns of the essential taboos to be respected, and the evil ones are vanquished. Each one of these ingredients and incidents, in the same order and down to the detail of the ball-game being the cause of the trouble, is preserved in the Scottish version of* Childe Rowland, *recited by a tailor in 1770 and preserved in the version given here by the folklorist Joseph Jacobs. As if this were not enough, Childe Rowland also has illustrious literary relationships. In addition to Shakespeare's reference, Browning wrote a poem with this*

title; and the plot of the story is almost identical with that of Milton's Comus. *Jacobs noted the affinity with* Comus *in 1899, and averred that the resemblance could hardly be a coincidence. He would perhaps have been equally surprised if he had noted the South American version. It was published by Spence in 1913, and although Jacobs died in 1916, apparently he did not see it. When I mentioned the resemblance to Lewis Spence in the nineteen-forties, he had not seen Jacobs' version either.*

Childe Rowland and his brothers twain
Were playing at the ball,
And there was their sister Burd Ellen
In the midst, among them all.
Childe Rowland kicked it with his foot
And caught it with his knee;
At last he plunged among them all
O'er the church he made it flee.
Burd Ellen round about the aisle
To seek the ball is gone
But long they waited, and longer still,
And she came not back again.
They sought her east, they sought her west,
They sought her up and down,
And woe were the hearts of those brethren,
For she was not to be found.

So at last her elder brother went to the Warlock Merlin, the magician, told him all, and asked him if he knew where Burd Ellen was. 'The fair Burd Ellen,' said the Warlock Merlin, 'must have been carried off by the fairies, because she went round the church "widershins" – the opposite way to the sun. She is now in the Dark Tower of the King of Elfland; it would take the boldest knight in Christendom to bring her back.'

'If it is possible to bring her back,' said her brother, 'I'll do it, or perish in the attempt.'

'Possible it is,' said the Warlock Merlin, 'but woe

to the man, or mother's son that attempts it, if he is not well taught beforehand what he is to do.'

The eldest brother of Burd Ellen was not to be put off by any fear of danger, from attempting to get her back, so he begged the Warlock Merlin to tell him what he should do, and what he should not do, in going to seek his sister. And after he had been taught, and had repeated his lesson, he set out for Elfland.

But long they waited, and longer still,
With muckle doubt and pain,
But woe were the hearts of his brethren,
For he came not back again.

Then the second brother got tired of waiting, and he went to the Warlock Merlin and asked him the same as his brother. So he set out to find Burd Ellen.

But long they waited, and longer still,
With muckle doubt and pain,
And woe were his mother's and brother's heart,
For he came not back again.

And when they had waited and waited a good long time, Childe Rowland, the youngest of Burd Ellen's brothers, wished to go, and went to his mother, the good Queen, to ask her to let him go. But she would not at first, for he was the last and dearest of her children; and if he were lost, all would be lost. But he begged, and he begged, till at last the good Queen let him go; and gave him his father's good brand [sword] that never struck in vain, and as she girt it round his waist, she said the spell that would give it victory.

So Childe Rowland said goodbye to the good Queen, his mother, and went to the cave of the Warlock Merlin. 'Once more, and but once more,' he said to the Warlock, 'tell how man or mother's son may rescue Burd Ellen and her brothers twain.'

'Well, my son,' said the Warlock Merlin, 'there are but two things, simple they may seem, but hard they are to do. One thing to do, and one thing not to do. And the thing you do is this: after you have entered the land of Fairy, whoever speaks to you, till you meet the Burd Ellen, you must out with your father's brand and off with their head. And what you've not to do is this: bite no bit, and drink no drop, however hungry or thirsty you be; drink a drop, or bite a bit, while in Elfland you be, and never will you see Middle Earth again.'

So Childe Rowland said the two things over and over again, till he knew them by heart, and he thanked the Warlock Merlin and went on his way. And he went along, and along, and still further along, till he came to the horse-herd of the King of Elfland feeding his horses. These he knew by their fiery eyes, and knew that he was at last in the land of the Fairy. 'Can'st thou tell me,' said Childe Rowland to the horse-herd, 'where the King of Elfland's Dark Tower is?'

'I cannot tell thee,' said the horse-herd, 'but go on a little further and thou wilt come to the cow-herd, and he, maybe, can tell thee.'

Then, without a word more, Childe Rowland drew the good brand that never struck in vain, and off went the horse-herd's head, and Childe Rowland went on further, till he came to the cow-herd, and asked him the same question. 'I can't tell thee,' said he, 'but go on a little further, and thou wilt come to the hen-wife, and she is sure to know.'

Then Childe Rowland out with his good brand, that never struck in vain, and off went the cow-herd's head. And he went on a little further, till he came to an old woman in a grey cloak, and he asked her if she knew where the Dark Tower of the King of Elfland was. 'Go on a little further,' said the hen-wife, 'till you come to a round green hill, surrounded with terrace-rings, from the bottom to the top – go round it three times "widershins", and each time say:

'"Open, door! open, door!
And let me come in."

'And the third time the door will open, and you may go in.'

And Childe Rowland was just going on, when he remembered what he had to do; so he out with the good brand, that never struck in vain, and off went the hen-wife's head.

Then he went on, and on, till he came to the round green hill with the terrace-rings from top to bottom, and he went round it three times, 'widershins', saying each time:

'Open, door, open!

And let me come in.'

And the third time the door did open, and he went in, and it closed with a click, and Childe Rowland was left in the gloom.

It was not exactly dark, but a kind of twilight or gloaming. There were neither windows nor candles and he could not make out where the twilight came from, if not through the walls and roof. These were rough arches made of a transparent rock, encrusted with sheepsilver and rockspar, and other bright stones. But though it was rock, the air was quite warm, as it always is in Elfland. So he went through this passage till at last he came to two wide and high folding doors which stood ajar. And when he opened them, there he saw a most wonderful and gracious sight. A large and spacious hall, so large it seemed to be as long, and as broad, as the green hill itself. The roof was supported by fine pillars, so large and lofty that the pillars of a cathedral were as nothing to them. They were all of gold and silver, with fretted work, and between them and around them wreaths of flowers, composed of diamonds and emeralds, and all manner of precious stones. And the very keystones of the arches had for ornaments clusters of diamonds and rubies, and pearls, and other precious stones. And all these arches met in the middle of the roof, and just there, hung by a golden chain, an immense lamp made out of one big pearl hollowed out and quite transparent. And in the middle of this was a big, huge carbuncle gem, which kept spinning round and round, and this was what gave light by its rays to the whole hall, which seemed as if the setting sun was shining on it.

The hall was furnished in a manner equally grand, and at one end of it was a glorious couch of velvet, silk and gold, and there sat Burd Ellen, combing her golden hair with a silver comb. And when she saw Childe Rowland, she stood up and said:

'God pity ye, poor luckless fool,
What have ye here to do?
Hear ye this, my youngest brother,
Why didn't ye bide at home?
Had you a hundred thousand lives
Ye couldn't spare any a one.
But sit ye down; but woe, O, woe,
That ever ye were born,
For come the King of Elfland in,
Your fortune is forlorn.'

Then they sat down together, and Childe Rowland told her all that he had done, and she told him how their two brothers had reached the Dark Tower, but had been enchanted by the King of Elfland, and lay there entombed as if dead. And then after they had talked a little longer Childe Rowland began to feel hungry from his long travels, and told his sister Burd

Ellen how hungry he was and asked for some food, forgetting all about the Warlock Merlin's warning.

Burd Ellen looked at Childe Rowland sadly, and shook her head, but she was under a spell, and could not warn him. So she rose up, and went out, and soon brought back a golden basin full of bread and milk. Childe Rowland was just going to raise it to his lips, when he looked at his sister and remembered why he had come all that way. So he dashed the bowl to the ground, and said: 'Not a sup will I swallow, nor a bit will I bite, till Burd Ellen is set free.'

Just at that moment they heard the noise of someone approaching, and a loud voice was heard saying:

'Fee, fi, fo, fum,

I smell the blood of a Christian man,

Be he dead, be he living, with my brand,

I'll dash his brains from his brain-pan.'

And then the folding doors of the hall were burst open, and the King of Elfland rushed in.

'Strike then, Bogie [goblin], if you darest,' shouted out Childe Rowland, and rushed to meet him with his good brand that never yet did fail. They fought, and they fought, and they fought, till Childe Rowland beat the King of Elfland down on his knees, and caused him to yield and beg for mercy. 'I grant thee mercy,' said Childe Rowland; 'release my sister from thy spells and raise my brothers to life, and let us all go free, and thou shalt be spared.'

'I agree,' said the Elfin King, and rising up he went to a chest from which he took a phial filled with a blood-red liquor. With this he anointed the ears, eyelids, nostrils, lips and finger-tips of the two brothers, and they sprang at once into life, and declared that their souls had been away, but had now returned. The Elfin King then said some words to Burd Ellen, and she was disenchanted, and they all four passed out of the hall, through the long passage, and turned their back on the Dark Tower, never to return again. So they reached home and the good Queen their mother and Burd Ellen never went round a church 'widershins' again.

The Tale of Mushkil Gusha

Traditional tales were felt, in the 18th century, to be 'an affront to the rational mind' as the illustrious Iona and Peter Opie remind us in The Classic Fairy Tales *(London: Oxford University Press, 1974). Nowadays, of course, the work of psychologists makes people more open-minded, sometimes even to the point of agreeing with the famous folklorist Joseph Campbell that the folktale is 'the primer of the picture-language of the soul'.*

Never having been through a phase of believing in the complete sovereignty of the intellect at the expense of other sides of humanity, people in the East have for long regarded certain traditional stories as having a real function, and effect on the mind and on the community.

Such a tale is that which is sometimes called 'The Tale of Mushkil Gusha – the Remover of All Difficulties'. It is known in both major and minor communities in India and Pakistan, in Central Asia and Iran, in the Near East and even in Africa and the Yemens. It is believed that if this story is recited on Thursday nights, it will in some inexplicable way help the work of the mysterious Mushkil Gusha, Friend of Man.

ONCE UPON A time, not a thousand miles from here, there lived a poor old wood-cutter, who was a widower, and his little daughter. Every day he used to go into the mountains to cut firewood, which he brought home and tied into bundles. Then he used to have breakfast and walk into the nearest town, where he would sell his wood and rest for a time before returning home.

One day, when he reached home very late, the girl said to him, 'Father, I sometimes wish that we could have some nicer food, and more and different kinds of things to eat.'

'Very well, my child,' said the old man; 'tomorrow I shall get up much earlier than I usually do. I shall go further into the mountains where there is more wood, and I shall bring back a much larger quantity than usual. I will get home earlier and I will be able to bundle the wood sooner, and I will go into town and sell it so that we can have more money and I shall bring you back all kinds of nice things to eat.'

The next morning the wood-cutter rose before dawn and went into the mountains. He worked very hard cutting wood and trimming it and made it into a huge bundle which he carried on his back to his little house.

When he got home, it was still very early. He put his load of wood down, and knocked on the door, saying, 'Daughter, Daughter, open the door, for I am hungry and thirsty and I need a meal before I go to market.'

But the door was locked. The wood-cutter was so tired that he lay down and was soon fast asleep beside his bundle. The little girl, having forgotten all about their conversation the night before, was fast asleep in bed. When he woke up a few hours later, the sun was high. The wood-cutter knocked on the door again and said, 'Daughter, Daughter, come quickly; I must have a little food and go to market to sell the wood; for it is already much later than my usual time of starting.'

But, having forgotten all about the conversation, the little girl had meanwhile got up, tidied the house, and gone out for a walk. She had locked the door assuming in her forgetfulness that her father was still in the town.

So the wood-cutter thought to himself, 'It is now rather late to go into the town, I will therefore return to the mountains and cut another bundle of wood, which I will bring home, and tomorrow I will take a double load to market.'

All that day the old man toiled in the mountains cutting wood and shaping the branches. When he got home with the wood on his shoulders, it was evening.

He put down his burden behind the house, knocked on the door and said, 'Daughter, Daughter, open the door for I am tired and I have eaten nothing all day. I have a double bundle of wood which I hope to take to market tomorrow. Tonight I must sleep well so that I will be strong.'

But there was no answer, for the little girl when she came home had felt very sleepy, and had made a meal for herself and gone to bed. She had been rather worried at first that her father was not home, but she decided that he must have arranged to stay in town overnight.

Once again the wood-cutter, finding that he could not get into the house, tired, hungry and thirsty, lay down by his bundles of wood and fell fast asleep. He could not keep awake, although he was fearful for what might have happened to the little girl.

Now the wood-cutter, because he was so cold and hungry and tired, woke very, very early the next morning: before it was even light.

He sat up, and looked around, but he could not see anything. And then a strange thing happened. The wood-cutter thought he heard a voice saying: 'Hurry, hurry! Leave your wood and come this way. If you need enough, and you want little enough, you shall have delicious food.'

The wood-cutter stood up and walked in the direction of the voice. And he walked and he walked; but he found nothing.

By now he was colder and hungrier and more tired than ever, and he was lost. He had been full of hope, but that did not seem to have helped him. Now he felt sad, and he wanted to cry. But he realised that crying would not help him either, so he lay down and fell asleep.

Quite soon he woke up again. It was too cold, and he was too hungry, to sleep. So he decided to tell himself, as if in a story, everything that had happened to him since his little daughter had first said that she wanted a different kind of food.

As soon as he had finished his story, he thought he heard another voice, saying, somewhere above him, out of the dawn, 'Old man, what are you doing sitting there?'

'I am telling myself my own story,' said the wood-cutter.

'And what is that?' said the voice.

The old man repeated his tale. 'Very well,' said the voice. And then it told the old wood-cutter to close his eyes and to mount as it were, a step. 'But I do not see any step,' said the old man. 'Never mind, but do as I say,' said the voice.

The old man did as he was told. As soon as he had closed his eyes, he found that he was standing up and as he raised his right foot he felt that there was something like a step under it. He started to ascend what seemed to be a staircase. Suddenly the whole flight of steps started to move, very fast, and the voice said, 'Do not open your eyes until I tell you to do so.'

In a very short time, the voice told the old man to open his eyes. When he did he found that he was in a place which looked rather like a desert, with the sun beating down on him. He was surrounded by masses and masses of pebbles; pebbles of all colours: red, green, blue and white. But he seemed to be alone. He looked all around him, and could not see anyone, but the voice started to speak again.

'Take up as many of these stones as you can,' said the voice, 'then close your eyes, and walk down the steps once more.'

The wood-cutter did as he was told, and he found himself, when he opened his eyes again at the voice's bidding, standing before the door of his own house.

He knocked at the door and his little daughter answered it. She asked him where he had been, and he told her, although she could hardly understand what he was saying, it all sounded so confusing.

They went into the house, and the little girl and her father shared the last food which they had, which was a handful of dried dates.

When they had finished, the old man thought that he heard a voice speaking to him again, a voice just like the other one which had told him to climb the stairs.

The voice said, 'Although you may not know it yet, you have been saved by Mushkil Gusha. Remember that Mushkil Gusha is always here. Make sure that every Thursday night you eat some dates and give some to any needy person, and tell the story of Mushkil Gusha. Or give a gift in the name of Mushkil Gusha to someone who will help the needy. Make sure that the story of Mushkil Gusha is never, never forgotten. If you do this, and if this is done by those to whom you tell the story, the people who are in real need will always find their way.'

The wood-cutter put all the stones which he had brought back from the desert in a corner of his little house. They looked very much like ordinary stones, and he did not know what to do with them.

The next day he took his two enormous bundles of wood to market, and sold them easily for a high price. When he got home he took his daughter all sorts of delicious kinds of food, which she had never tasted before. And when they had eaten it, the old woodcutter said: 'Now I am going to tell you the whole story of Mushkil Gusha. Mushkil Gusha is "the remover of all difficulties". Our difficulties have been removed through Mushkil Gusha and we must always remember it.'

For nearly a week after that the old man carried on as usual. He went into the mountains, brought back wood, had a meal, took the wood to market and sold it. He always found a buyer without difficulty.

Now the next Thursday came, and, as is the way of men, the wood-cutter forgot to repeat the tale of Mushkil Gusha.

Late that evening, in the house of the wood-cutter's neighbours, the fire had gone out. The neighbours had nothing with which to re-light the fire, and they went to the house of the wood-cutter. They said, 'Neighbour, neighbour, please give us a light from those wonderful lamps of yours which we see shining through the window.'

'What lamps?' said the wood-cutter.

'Come outside,' said the neighbours, 'and see what we mean.'

So the wood-cutter went outside and then he saw, sure enough, all kinds of brilliant lights shining through the window from the inside.

He went back to the house, and saw that the light was streaming from the pile of pebbles which he had put in the corner. But the rays of light were cold, and it was not possible to use them to light a fire. So he went out to the neighbours and said, 'Neighbours, I am sorry, I have no fire.' And he banged the door in their faces. They were annoyed and confused, and went back to their house, muttering. They leave our story here.

The wood-cutter and his daughter quickly covered up the brilliant lights with every piece of cloth they could find, for fear that anyone would see what a treasure they had. The next morning, when they uncovered the stones, they discovered that they were precious, luminous gems.

They took the jewels, one by one, to neighbouring towns, where they sold them for a huge price. Now the wood-cutter decided to build for himself and for his daughter a wonderful palace. They chose a site just opposite the castle of the King of their country. In a very short time a marvellous building had come into being.

Now that particular King had a beautiful daughter, and one day when she got up in the morning, she saw a sort of fairy-tale castle just opposite her father's and she was amazed. She asked her servants, 'Who has built this castle? What right have these people to do such a thing so near to our home?'

The servants went away and made enquiries and they came back and told the story, as far as they could collect it, to the Princess.

The Princess called for the little daughter of the wood-cutter, for she was very angry with her, but when the two girls met and talked they soon became fast friends. They started to meet every day and went to swim and play in the stream which had been made for the Princess by her father. A few days after they first met, the Princess took off a beautiful and valuable necklace and hung it up on a tree just beside the stream. She forgot to take it down when they came out of the water, and when she got home she thought it must have been lost.

The Princess thought a little and then decided

that the daughter of the wood-cutter had stolen her necklace. So she told her father, and he had the wood-cutter arrested; he confiscated the castle and declared forfeit everything that the wood-cutter had. The old man was thrown into prison, and the daughter was put into an orphanage.

As was the custom in that country, after a period of time the wood-cutter was taken from the dungeon and put in the public square, chained to a post, with a sign around his neck. On the sign was written: 'This is what happens to those who steal from Kings'.

At first people gathered around him, and jeered and threw things at him. He was most unhappy.

But quite soon, as is the way of men, everyone became used to the sight of the old man sitting there by his post, and took very little notice of him. Sometimes people threw him scraps of food, sometimes they did not.

One day he overheard somebody saying that it was Thursday afternoon. Suddenly, the thought came into his mind that it would soon be the evening of Mushkil Gusha, the remover of all difficulties, and that he had forgotten to commemorate him for so many days. No sooner had this thought come into his head, than a charitable man, passing by, threw him a tiny coin. The wood-cutter called out: 'Generous friend, you have given me money, which is of no use to me. If, however, your kindness could extend to buying one or two dates and coming and sitting and eating them with me, I would be eternally grateful to you.'

The other man went and bought a few dates. And they sat and ate them together. When they had finished, the wood-cutter told the other man the story of Mushkil Gusha. 'I think you must be mad,' said the generous man. But he was a kindly person who himself had many difficulties. When he arrived home after this incident, he found that all his problems had disappeared. And that made him start to think a great deal about Mushkil Gusha. But he leaves our story here.

The very next morning the Princess went back to her bathing-place. As she was about to go into the water, she saw what looked like her necklace down at the bottom of the stream. As she was going to dive in to try to get it back, she happened to sneeze. Her head went up, and she saw that what she had thought was the necklace was only its reflection in the water. It was hanging on the bough of the tree where she had left it such a long time before. Taking the necklace down, the Princess ran excitedly to her father and told him what had happened. The King gave orders for the wood-cutter to be released and given a public apology. The little girl was brought back from the orphanage, and everyone lived happily ever after.

These are some of the incidents in the story of

Mushkil Gusha. It is a very long tale and it is never ended. It has many forms. Some of them are even not called the story of Mushkil Gusha at all, so people do not recognise it. But it is because of Mushkil Gusha that his story, in whatever form, is remembered by somebody, somewhere in the world, day and night, wherever there are people. As his story had always been recited, so it will always continue to be told.

The Food of Paradise

What does a folktale really mean? Scholars and others take them to pieces; ideologues look for those which will support their beliefs about tales; literary people often use them as the basis for their own works. Folktales are recited, in many cultures, by professional or at any rate highly expert specialists: and these are sometimes only superannuated and toothless grandmothers. In spite of the enormous amount of work done on the collection, analysis and study of tales, how many collectors have troubled themselves to ask the reciters themselves, the experts, what the tale is supposed to mean, or what effect it is intended to have? I asked a Central Asian bard this question, for he had contributed several hundred tales to an 'ethnographic mission'. He said: 'This is one thing I was never asked by the learned men and women.'

His explanation of the function of this tale, 'The Food of Paradise', is that it will confirm the bias of those who, for example, believe that humility is really living off the by-products of a total system. It will also, he continued, encourage those who think that even those things which seem wonderful (the sweetmeat) are as nothing, seen from a wider perspective. 'But,' he continued, 'for those who are ready to understand the truth: they will find this tale valuable to take them beyond such simple confirmations.'

ON THE CLOSE of my visit to the Holy City Mecca, I joined the caravan of Sheikh Amru, who apart from being a great theological teacher, was a famous narrator of ancient tales. The occasion was when he asked me as to what calling I was going to choose after my wanderings. Somewhat humorously I said that I was going to do nothing for my living since Allah has promised to feed the Faithful.

'Listen my son,' said the Sheikh, as he reclined against his camel's saddle; and then I knew that an ancient tale was to be retailed out to us. This is what he said:

In the school founded by the Caliph for the study of divine things sat the devout Mullah Ibrahim, his hands folded in his lap, in an attitude of meditation. Ibrahim taught students from all the countries of Islam, but the work was thankless and ill-paid. And as he sat there he thought on his state for the first time in many years.

'Why is it,' he said to himself, 'that a man so holy as I am must toil so hard to instruct a pack of blockheads, when others who have merited nothing through piety or attention to the Commands of Allah fare sumptuously every day and neither toil nor spin? O, Compassionate One, is not this thing unjust? Whereof should Thy servant be burdened, like an ass in the market-place, which carries two panniers, both filled to the top, and stumbles at every blow of the driver's stick?'

And as he considered, Ibrahim the Wise, as men called him, brought to mind that verse in the Holy Literature in which it says: 'Allah will not let any one starve.' And taking deeper counsel with himself, he said: 'May it not be that those whom I have blamed for their sloth and inactivity are, after all, the better Moslems, that they have greater faith than I? For, perusing this passage, they may have said to themselves: "I will cast myself upon the mercy of Allah, which in this text is surely extended to all men. Allah in his bounty will surely feed and maintain me." Why then toil and strive as the faithless do? It is those who have faith that are the elect.'

At that moment a great pasha halted before the gates of the seminary, in his piety alighting from his palanquin to give alms to a beggar, as all good Muslims do. And as Ibrahim watched him through the lattice, he thought: 'Does not the condition of the beggar as well as that of this pasha prove the justice of the text upon which I have been meditating? Neither starves, but the wealthier man is assuredly the more devout, for he is the giver and not the receiver, and for this very purpose has been blest with the goods of this world. Why do I hesitate, wretched man that I am? Shall I not, as the Book ordains, cast myself on the bounty of Allah and free myself forever from the intolerable burden of instructing fools in a wisdom they can never understand?'

So saying, Ibrahim the Sage arose from his place in the College of the Caliph, and walked out of the City of Baghdad where he had dwelt for many years. It was evening, and betaking himself to the banks of the river, he selected a dry and shady spot beneath a spreading cypress tree, and awaiting the bounty of Allah, fell fast asleep in the certainty that the Lord of all Compassion would not fail him.

When he awoke, it was early morning, and a divine hush lay upon everything. Ibrahim lazily speculated as to the manner in which he would be sustained. Would the birds of the air bring him sustenance, would the fishes from the stream leap ashore, offering themselves for the assuagement of his growing hunger? In what way did those who merited the help of Allah first receive it, if not in some miraculous manner? True, the wealthy were bequeathed riches by their parents. But there must be a beginning. A pasha might sail down the river in his barge and supply his wants out of golden dishes and silver cups.

But morning blossomed into day, and day into night, and still the miracle remained unaccomplished. More than one pasha glided past him in his gilded barge, but these made only the customary salutations and gave no other sign. On the road above, pilgrims and travellers passed, but without taking the least notice of him. Hunger gnawed at his vitals, and he thought with envy of the millet porridge with goats' milk which the mullahs would now be enjoying at the seminary. Still was he trustful, and, as he made the customary ablutions in the river, his faith had abated not one jot.

Again he slept, and once more day dawned in scarlet and silver beauty. By this time he felt so faint as scarcely to be able to stand. The hours crept slowly onward, yet no sign came that his hunger was to be satisfied.

At last, as midday approached with its stifling heat, something floating on the surface of the water caught his eye. It seemed like a mass of leaves wrapped up with fibre; and, wading into the river, he succeeded in catching it. Back he splashed with his prize to the bank, and sitting down on the sward, he opened the packet. It contained a quantity of the most delicious-looking halwa, that famous marzipan, of whose making only Baghdad knows the secret, a sweetmeat composed of sugar mingled with paste of almonds and attar of roses and other delicate and savoury essences.

After gorging himself with the delightful fare, Ibrahim the Wise drank deeply from the river, and lolled on the grass, sure that his prayer had been answered, and that he would never have to toil more. There was sufficient of the ambrosial food to serve for three meals a day; and on each day, after the hour of midday prayer, a similar packet of halwa came floating down the stream as though placed there by the hands of angels.

'Surely,' said the Mullah, 'the promises of Allah are true, and the man who trusts in Him will not be deceived. Truly I did well to leave the seminary, where, day-in, day-out, I had perforce to cram divine knowledge into the heads of idiots incapable of repeating a verse correctly even at the fifteenth attempt.'

Months passed, and Ibrahim continued to receive the food that Allah had promised with unfailing regularity. Then, quite naturally, he began to speculate whence it came. If he could find the spot where it was deposited on the surface of the stream, surely he must witness a miracle, and as he had never done so, he felt greatly desirous of attaining the merit such a consummation would undoubtedly add to his repute as a holy man.

So one morning, after eating the last of the halwa he had received the preceding day, he girded up his loins, and taking his staff, began slowly to walk upstream.

'Now,' said he, 'if what I suppose be true, I will today receive my luscious food at an earlier hour than usual, as I shall be nearer the place where it is placed on the water and indeed on each day I shall receive at an even earlier hour, until at last I come to the spot where some divine seraph, sent by Allah from Paradise, drops the savoury food of heaven upon the stream in justification of my trust in the most Merciful.'

For some days Ibrahim walked upstream, keeping carefully to the bank of the river and fixing his eyes on its surface in case he should fail to discern the packet of halwa. Every day, at an even earlier hour, it floated regularly past him, carried by the current so near to the shore that he could easily wade out and secure it. At nights he slept beneath a convenient tree, and as men perceived him to be a Mullah and a holy man, no one thought of molesting him.

It was on the fourth day of his journey that he observed the river had widened. In a large island in the midst of the stream rose a fair castle. The island comprised a princely domain of noble meadow-land and rich gardens, crossed and interlaced by the silver of narrow streams, and was backed by the blue and jagged peaks of great mountains. The castle itself was built of marble white as sculptured ice, and its green and shady lawns sloped down to a silent and extensive shore of golden sand.

And when night descended, this wondrous region was illuminated by the romance of moonlight into an almost unearthly radiance; so that Ibrahim, in all his piety, was forced to compare it with Paradise itself. The white castle on its dark rocks seemed like day pedestalled upon night, and from the sea-green of the shadow of myrtles rose the peaks of pavilions, whence came the sound of guitars and lutes and voices more ravishingly sweet than Ibrahim, the son of the seminary, had ever believed earth could hold.

And as Ibrahim gazed spellbound at the wondrous spectacle and drank in the sounds of ecstasy which arose from the garden, wondering whether he were not already dead and in the purlieus of Heaven, a harsh voice hailed him at his very elbow, asking him what he was doing there. He turned swiftly to see standing beside him an ancient man in the garb of a hermit, with long matted hair and tangled beard.

'Salaam, good father,' he said, much relieved, for like all men of peace, he feared violence. 'The peace of Allah, the Merciful, the Compassionate, be upon you.'

'And upon you, my son,' replied the anchorite. 'But what do you do here at this hour of the night, when all such as you should be asleep?'

'Like yourself, I am a holy man,' replied Ibrahim, with unction, 'but I travel on a quest the nature of which I may not divulge to any. Passing this spot, I was attracted by the unusual appearance of yonder castle and its surroundings, and would learn its history, if that is known to you.'

'It is, though in part only,' rejoined the hermit, 'for I have dwelt many years in this neighbourhood, but have little converse with men. Know, then, that the place you behold is called the Silver Castle. It was built by a Pasha now dead, who was greatly enamoured of a certain Princess, whose father refused him her hand in marriage. But, not to be gainsaid, so fierce and unruly a thing is love in some men, he built this strength in the midst of the river as you see, and placed upon it so many dark and terrible spells of magic that none could cross to or from it without his sanction. Then, abducting the Princess, he espoused her and placed her in yonder tower. The King, her father, came with an army to besiege the place, but so potent were the necromancies the Pasha had surrounded it with that he was compelled to raise the siege and leave his daughter in the hands of his enemy.'

'You amaze me,' cried Ibrahim. 'And does this Princess remain here still?'

'No, brother,' replied the hermit, 'like her lord she has passed away, but they have left behind them a daughter who governs the castle, a lady of surpassing beauty, who spends her days in pleasure and in spending the wealth her father bequeathed her. But she has but one sorrow, and that is that none can dissolve the spells woven by her father the Pasha, so that no one may either gain admittance to the castle or leave it. Her companions are therefore either the very aged or those born on the island and no other, which, for a young and beautiful woman, must be wearisome. But you will pardon me, brother, I am going on a pilgrimage to a certain shrine in Baghdad, where I betake myself once a year to acquire merit. Meanwhile if you choose to rest, you may dwell in my humble cell yonder until I return in seven days' time.'

Ibrahim gladly accepted the hermit's offer, and when he had gone, sat down to ponder over the tale he had told him. Now, among other wisdoms, he had acquired during his years of study a deep knowledge of the magical art, and he bethought him that it might be given to him to rid the castle and the inhabitants of the spells which held them prisoner on the island.

But in the midst of his thoughts he fell asleep, and did not waken until the sun was high in the heavens. Then he made his ablutions, and betook himself to the bank of the river, where he sat and watched the surface of the water for a sign of the appearance of the delicious food he received daily.

And as he watched, he beheld a curious thing. Some three hours before midday, a very beautiful woman appeared on the marble battlements which overhung the river. So fair was she that the Mullah gasped with surprise at the radiance of her beauty, which was that of the houris of Paradise. For her hair was as golden wire which is drawn thin by the cunning of the goldsmith, her eyes were yellow, and bright as topazes found on Mount Ararat, and the colour of her cheeks was as that of the roses of Isfahan. And as for the flesh of her body, it shone with the lustre of

80

silver, so brightly polished it was.

'Can this be the Princess,' thought Ibrahim, 'or an angel from heaven? Nay, surely it is she, for this woman, though surpassingly beautiful, is still a mortal.'

And as Ibrahim stood beholding her, she raised her arm and cast something into the river. And when she had done so, she withdrew from the battlements and disappeared like a star behind clouds.

The Mullah kept his eyes fixed on what she had cast into the stream, and in a little perceived that it was the very packet of leaves which he was wont to receive daily. Wading into the stream, he secured it, unwrapped it, and found it full of the delicious halwa, as usual.

'Ha,' said he, as he devoured the savoury sweetmeat. 'So now I know at last that radiant being by whose hands Allah, the Just, the Merciful, has ordained I shall be fed daily. Truly, the Compassionate must have put it into the heart of this divine princess to cast this luscious food on the breast of the stream at the self-same hour each day. And shall I not seek to repay her the distinguished kindness she has done me by freeing her from the spells by which she is encompassed, and which keep her a prisoner, she who should be wed to a Sultan at least and should reign in Baghdad itself?'

And with these grateful thoughts, he sat down to consider by what means the spells which surrounded the castle might be broken. Casting himself into a deep trance, he walked in spirit in the Land of the Jinn, where as a holy man, he could come to no harm. And coming to the house of one of the Jinn, whom he knew and whose name was Adhem, he summoned him and had speech with him.

'Hail, holy man,' said Adhem, making low obeisance. 'I am your servant. In what way can I serve you?'

Ibrahim acquainted him with the reason for his presence there, at which the Jinn assumed an air of the greatest concern.

'What you ask is indeed hard, most wise Ibrahim,' he said doubtfully. 'But I will take counsel of my brethren on the matter without delay, and shall let you know the result of our deliberations by a speedy and trusty messenger. No more can I say or do at present.'

With this Ibrahim departed and soon after awoke from his trance. He seemed only to have been an hour in the Land of the Jinn, but it must have been five hours or more, for the sun was high in the heavens when he fell asleep, and now the moonlight was sparkling on the waters of the river. And the same exquisite music he had heard before arose from the gardens of the castle, as though from the lips of peris.

And as Ibrahim listened, entranced, a shape scarcely more solid than the moonlight rose slowly out of the river and stood before him in the shadowy likeness of a Jinn. Three times it made obeisance before him, then it spoke.

'Most wise and holy Ibrahim,' it said, 'my master Adhem, a prince among the people of the Jinn, has sent me to acquaint you with the decision of his counsellors. They proffer you this ring set with the diamond which men call adamant, and in whose shining surface if you will gaze, you shall behold the nature of those spells which keep the Princess and her people prisoners in yonder castle. And, having discovered the nature of those spells, if you summon our people to your aid in such shapes as will dissolve or break them, they will come in such guise as will set the Princess free.'

With those words the Jinn vanished into the river whence he had come. And, without delay, Ibrahim took the ring which the spirit had cast on the grass at his feet, and peered into the shining stone it held.

And straightaway he beheld the first spell. Close to the shore of the river arose a mighty bastion as of stone, invisible to mortal eyes, which surrounded the castle from shore to shore. And Ibrahim summoned to him the hosts of the Jinns in the guise of sappers, with picks and hammers, and on this wall they fell mightily in their myriads, so that without sound or clamour of any sort, they reduced it to dust ere a man could count a hundred.

Then Ibrahim looked once more in the surface of

the diamond and saw a great web like that of a spider hanging in the air round the castle. And he summoned the hosts of the Jinn in the shape of eagles, which so rent the invisible web with their strong beaks that in almost less time than it takes to tell of it, it fell in fragments into the stream.

Once more Ibrahim gazed into the stone, and this time he saw an army of sightless giants, with spear and scimitar in hand, drawn up in array of war on the shores of the island. And he called the Jinn people to him in the likeness of greater and more powerful giants, who did battle with those on the island. Terrible was the strife, and Ibrahim trembled mightily as he watched it. But soon the Jinn prevailed over the giants of the island, and put them to flight.

The spells which had surrounded the castle were now removed, and as day had dawned, Ibrahim cast about for some means of reaching the castle. No sooner had he wished this than by the power of the Jinn a bridge rose out of the stream by which he was enabled to cross to the island. And when he had done so, he was accosted by an old man who held a bared scimitar in his hand, and who asked him by what means he had been enabled to reach the island, which had so long been under enchantment.

'That I may tell only to your lady, the Princess,' said Ibrahim. 'Admit me to her presence without delay.'

The guard, marvelling, ushered him through

the great gate of the castle, and across a spacious court where fountains sang mellifluously. Entering a magnificent hall, whose floor was inlaid with squares of blue and white marble and the walls with lapis lazuli and other rare stones, he gave the Mullah into the keeping of a black eunuch, who requested the holy man to follow him.

Upon a dais sat the incomparable Princess whom Ibrahim had beheld on the battlements, and who daily cast the packet of halwa on the waters of the river. To her the Mullah made obeisance, and, kneeling before her, told his tale.

'And what, most wise Ibrahim, do you ask in recompense of your so notable offices on my behalf?' asked the Princess. 'Speak, and it shall be granted to you, even to the half of my inheritance.'

'Nay, noble lady,' exclaimed Ibrahim. 'For have I not reason enough to be grateful to your Highness for the delicious food with which you have fed me daily? That halwa which you cast every morning from the battlements, and which has floated downstream, I have eaten with thankfulness. Surely only an angel from Paradise could have put it into your heart to despatch it.'

The Princess blushed so deeply that her heightened colour could be seen even beneath her veil.

'Alas, good Mullah!' she cried, wringing her hands. 'What is this you tell me? Curses on the day on which

I first cast that halwa, as you call it, on the waters of the river. Know, that each morning it is my custom to take a bath of milk, after which I anoint and rub my limbs with essence of almonds, sugar and sweet-scented cosmetics. These, then, I remove from my nakedness and, wrapping them in leaves, cast them into the stream.'

'Ah, now Princess, I see who has been blind,' cried Ibrahim, with a wry countenance. 'Allah surely gives food to everyone; but its quality and kind are dictated by what man deserves!'

The Lamb with the Golden Fleece

Although the first recorded literary appearance of the 'stick-fast' tale is in the Indian Jataka Tales, *traditionally dating from over two thousand years ago, it has only been traced in Western writings to a 15th Century English poem, 'The Tale of the Basin'.*

To the American Blacks goes the credit of carrying the oral version from Africa to the United States, where it may have arrived centuries before Joel Chandler Harris made it famous in 'The Wonderful Tar-Baby Story' in 1881. The tale is, in one form or another, known all over Europe and the Middle East. It was taken to Canada through French influence, and from there, probably, to three or four eastern American-Indian tribes. These Indians have supplied at least twenty-three variants of the tale.

A. M. Espinosa, reviewing over 150 versions, has plotted the three main routes westwards, affording valuable information about the way in which stories are diffused. By the study of the content of the versions, he found that one route was India–Africa–America; a second was India–Europe–Iberia–America and the third was India–Europe–American colonies.

Although some scholars have believed that many tales are found so widely apart because of polygenesis, the 'stick-fast' concept seems so very odd that it could be used as an argument against the polygenetic hypothesis.

THERE WAS ONCE a poor man who had a son, and as the son grew up his father sent him out to look for work. The son travelled about looking for a place, and at last met with a man who arranged to take him as a shepherd.

Next day his master gave him a flute, and sent him out with the sheep to see whether he was fit for his work. The lad never lay down all day, very unlike many lazy fellows. He drove his sheep from place to place and played his flute all day long.

There was among the sheep a lamb with golden fleece, which, whenever it heard the flute, began to dance. The lad became very fond of this lamb, and made up his mind not to ask any wages of his master but only this little lamb.

In the evening he returned home; his master waited at the gate; and, when he saw the sheep all there and all well-fed, he was very pleased, and began to bargain with the lad, who said he wished for nothing but the lamb with the golden fleece.

The farmer was very fond of the lamb himself, and it was with great unwillingness he promised it; but he gave in afterwards when he saw what a good servant the lad made.

The year passed away; the lad received the lamb for his wages, and set off home with it. As they journeyed night set in just as he reached a village, so he went to a farmhouse to ask for a night's lodging.

There was a daughter in the house, who, when she saw the lamb with the golden fleece, determined to steal it. About midnight she arose, and lo! the minute she touched the lamb she stuck hard-and-fast to its fleece, so that when the lad got up he found her stuck to the lamb. He could not separate them, and as he could not leave his lamb, he took them both.

As he passed the third door from the house where he had spent the night, he took out his flute and began to play. Then the lamb began to dance; and, on its wool, the girl.

Round a corner a woman was putting bread into the oven; looking up she saw the lamb dancing; and, on its wool, the girl. Seizing the baker's shovel in order to frighten the girl, she rushed out and shouted, 'Get away home with you, don't make such a fool of yourself.'

As the girl continued dancing, the woman called out, 'What, won't you obey?' and gave her a blow on her back with the shovel, which at once stuck to the girl, and the woman to the shovel, and the lamb carried them all off.

As they went on they came to the church. Here the lad began to play again, the lamb began to dance, and on the lamb's fleece the girl, and on the girl's back the shovel, and at the end of the shovel the woman.

Just then the priest was coming out from matins, and seeing what was going on began to scold them, and bid them not to be so foolish and to go home. As words were of no avail, he hit the woman a sound whack on her back with his cane, when – to his surprise – the cane stuck to the woman, and he to the end of his cane.

With this nice company, the lad went on; and towards dark reached the royal borough and took lodgings at the end of the town with an old woman.

'What news is there?' said he.

The old woman told him they were in very great sorrow: for the King's daughter was very ill, and no physician could heal her, but if she could but be made to laugh she would be better at once. No one had as yet been able to make her smile; and moreover the King had issued that very day a proclamation stating that whoever made her laugh should have her for his wife, and share the royal power.

The lad with the lamb could scarcely wait till daylight, so anxious was he to try his fortune.

In the morning he presented himself to the King and stated his business and was very graciously received.

The daughter stood in the hall at the front of the house; the lad then began to play the flute, the lamb to dance, on the lamb's fleece the girl, on the girl's back the shovel, at the end of the shovel the woman, on the woman's back the cane, and at the end of the cane the priest.

When the princess saw this sight she burst out laughing, which made the lamb so glad that it shook everything off its back, and the lamb, the girl, the woman, and the priest each danced by themselves for joy.

The King married his daughter to the shepherd, the priest was made court-chaplain, the woman, court bakeress, and the girl, lady-in-waiting to the Princess. The wedding lasted from one Monday to the other Tuesday, and the whole land was in great joy, and if the strings of the fiddle hadn't broken they would have been dancing yet!

The Man with the Wen

In Europe, this tale is known as 'The Presents of the Little Folk', as collected by the Brothers Grimm in Germany; and it most usually features two hunchbacks. It is quite widely distributed in France and Italy, and Turkish and other versions are also known. The following presentation is interesting because it is found in a collection of tales of Japan dated 1664, and believed to date from a much earlier time there. The behaviour of the goblins, with their piping and dancing and tricks, seems very close to that of the Irish little folk. Indeed, a similar fiction is found in Ireland, where it is known as the Legend of Knockgrafton. Supporters of the migration theory have suggested that it dates from times when a Turanian tribe occupied Ireland, even before the Celts; though such a supposition is not essential to explain its diffusion.

ONCE LONG AGO, in old Japan, there was a man who spent his days trudging up and down the mountains collecting wood. This he used to burn, and to make charcoal, for he was unable to make a living in any other way. This unfortunate fellow thought that the gods were in some way displeased with him, for he had on his left cheek a large and disfiguring swelling: what people call a wen.

He had gone to many doctors, but whatever treatment they had prescribed had never been of any use. In fact, whatever medicine he tried, the wen grew larger and larger day by day. He was so distressed at his appearance, that he shunned other people, and gradually became more and more miserable. His wife tried to be cheerful about the matter and pretended to be unaware of it – the wen and the depression into which her husband was falling – however, in the end it made her hate him.

Their life as charcoal burners was not one of much happiness; and for all the wood he could gather, there seemed to be very little financial gain. The poor woman was seriously thinking of running away, back to her own village, and leaving him and his monstrous wen forever.

One day, with an uncomfortable bundle of wood on his back in an osier basket, the charcoal burner went slowly up the mountain track, fingering his wen with exploring fingers, positive that it was larger than the day before.

Suddenly, the thunder rolled, the lightning flashed, and heavy slanting rain began to fall.

'O Merciful Heaven,' he cried, 'so far from home and so little wood, and now this downpour. Where can I shelter?'

Stumbling and falling, half blinded, he was at the end of his strength, when his hands touched the bark of a hollow tree. Gratefully, he eased the basket off his thin shoulders, and covered the top with his wide hat. He saw that there was enough space for him to creep into the hollow of the ancient tree-trunk. There was scarcely a drop of rain on his head and shoulders as he crouched there, and he pulled his thin coat around him, removing his sandals to rest his aching feet. The thunder rolled and it seemed as if the world was about to crack into millions of pieces. But, as quickly as it had begun, the storm ceased. The charcoal burner fingered his wen, and was just about to creep out of the tree when he heard the tramp of feet. The rays of the setting sun played on a group of people who came marching along the mountain path, lighting them with a crimson glow.

'Whoever can they be?' wondered the man, quickly retrieving his sandals and slipping his feet into them. He still remained inside the tree hollow, for the sound of wild piping came to his ears. With staring eyes he gazed at a multitude of creatures; they were the strangest he had ever seen in his life. There must have been about a hundred of them, a troop of what he now realised were some sort of enchanted beings.

They were all of strange shapes; some were tall, covered with creepers, hung with curious beads. Others were small and shrunken like skeletons with phosphorus eyes, dancing disjointedly, yet with a gay abandon. Some had the mouths of crocodiles, snapping like castanets, keeping in time to the sound of drums almost martial in their rhythms. There were elves with one eye in the middle of their foreheads, dwarves with tremendous feet, all stamping and leaping along the mountain path in perfect time with the shrill piping and drumming. There were pale witches with long black hair, and huge dark giants, dressed in bearskins. Those who did not have musical instruments had magic wands in their hands, or claws, or paws; but each was leaping and pirouetting in joy and excitement. Some had two horns, some had only one, but each contributed noisily to the general merriment and air of carnival.

Not daring to show himself, the frightened charcoal burner peeped through a knothole, and held his breath. They came to a stop just near his hiding place, and the stamping and music grew louder.

They made a large circle, ambling or hopping, round and round, with one of their number in the middle (the head demon evidently) jumping as high as the others' heads in a series of extraordinary leaps. They lit a huge bonfire, and holding up torches which they ignited there, shouted and sang at the top of their voices.

The firelight gleamed on furry legs, shining tusks, or flashing eyes. As he watched, and heard the music, the charcoal burner became as gay as they. Forgotten was his wen, and his predicament; he leaped into the firelight and his feet carried him round in a most lively dance. His wen bobbed about, but he did not even try to cover it as usual with one hand. His arms were flung into the air, and he danced crazily, willing and fey, with all the others enjoying themselves round the fire.

'Well done! Excellent timing!' shouted the head demon. 'Keep it up, human being, we are much entertained!' Each demon roared or screeched encouragement.

The man danced like one whose very life depended on his feet not touching the ground for more than a split second.

The lesser demons piled more wood on the flames, others carried torches round and round. The laughter and screeching grew in intensity, and so did the intricate dancing of all present. The charcoal burner managed to hold his own in that mighty throng. He laughed as he had not done since the night of his wedding so many years ago, when he felt himself to be the happiest and most favoured man of the village where he was born.

At last, completely worn-out, he came to a sudden stop, and felt terribly thirsty. As if he had read the charcoal-burner's mind, the head demon handed him a bowl of wine. The flavour was amazingly good, and it slipped down his throat like a priceless elixir. He felt as good as ever within a few seconds of having drunk, and felt the gleaming eyes of the head demon upon him. 'You have danced well,' said the demon with sincerity. 'We have been immensely privileged to have you in our little company. Never have we seen a human who could keep up with our ideas of revelry, let alone surpass us!'

'No, no,' said the charcoal burner politely, 'it was most remarkably good of you to allow my faltering steps to…'

'Faltering steps! You are a master of the dance!' roared the demon, pressing the wine bowl upon the man once more. 'I speak for all of my people when I say we have tonight, in fact, learned much in the way of steps from you! You must come tomorrow night and teach us more.'

Very flattered by the important demon's attentions, the human being could scarcely believe his ears. 'Tomorrow night? Oh, Noble Entity. I would like nothing better in this world. Just let me recover my strength and I will with all my heart attend your revels here, for I am most amazed by your frivolity,' he answered gallantly.

'Just a moment though,' said the head demon, as his minions refilled his wine bowl, and lavished every attention on him. 'Human beings sometimes find life so demanding that they forget our invitations… Let us see what sort of a pledge you can leave with us so that we can be sure that you will come back.'

A few of the demons held a consultation, and when they had made a decision, they came to the head demon and said, 'Lord Demon, we have democratically decided that, as some humans consider a wen to be a very fortunate thing to have, we will ask the man to leave that as a sign of his good faith.'

'Done,' said the head demon, 'with your permission, good sir, of course, just a small prick!'

The charcoal burner's finger went up to his cheek in his usual gesture of dismay. He felt a minute twinge, as if a gnat had stung him, and at that moment the entire devilish company vanished. And, with them, his wen had also disappeared.

He could not believe his good fortune. The moon was now up, all signs of the fire the demons had lit and danced around had gone. He slipped his osier-basket onto his back, loaded with the wood he had collected, and made his way home with his mind in a turmoil.

His wife was delighted to see him, without the

monstrous wen. Her heart was uplifted, and she decided not to run away after all. Life would now be much better, with the hideous lump removed from her husband's face. He told her everything, from start to finish, and her eyes were like a faun's in the lamplight. All the love she had had for him on their wedding day returned. But more was to come. In the bottom of his osier-basket, when the wood was all taken out and stacked in the hut, were a hundred pieces of finest silver money.

'Husband! Husband! You will never have to work again collecting wood, we can enter some other, nice clean business. Let us give thanks to the gods for what they have caused to happen tonight!' cried the woman in the height of excitement.

Now, next morning, the tale was told all round the charcoal-burner's circle of friends. One neighbour, a baker, said:

'O, dear brother, let me go in your place, please, so that I could have this wen removed from my cheek, for it has plagued me greatly since it appeared a few months ago.

'If only I could go and meet those demons, the dancing would be quite easy to do, I'm sure, and I certainly could do with a hundred pieces of finest silver to get myself a new oven!' His wife added her screams and tears to his request.

So the kindly charcoal-burner told the baker

where to go, and the neighbour set off gaily up the mountain track. He reached the hollow tree, and settled down for a long wait, eating some salted fish and bread while he looked forward to the devilish train's arrival. He had a large osier-basket with him, in which he hoped to take his silver home. No sooner had the sun disappeared than he heard the tramp of the approaching throng. Pipes, flutes and drums grew louder and louder. Singing and shouting, the demons came, as before, into the clearing. Their heads tossed, their eyes and teeth gleamed in the starlight. The festivities began, the fire was lit, and the demons started dancing. Soon the whole mountainside was reverberating with sound.

'Has the man not come, as he promised he would?' some of the demons began to ask each other.

'Here I am, just as I agreed!' shouted the baker, running towards them. He took out his fan, and covering his wen, began to dance and sing as hard as he possibly could. But, his feet were not as nimble as that of the charcoal-burner, and he had no natural rhythm at all. He just seemed to shuffle and hop, with no more grace than a goat. The demons looked on with distaste, and several gave him the thumbs-down sign. The head demon snarled with rage as the man cavorted clumsily round the fire. 'Your feet are like lead, nothing like last night's performance!' he roared, and the others screeched insults, spitting at the baker like wildcats. 'This won't do, we are not at all amused by this behaviour. Where is your heart tonight? Here take your pledge and go, leave us this instant!' Thunder rolled, lightning flashed, rain fell. The roaring and offensive remarks hurled at him so terrified the baker that he ran for his life, a wen on either cheek.

The Skilful Brothers

This story has wandered across the world, perhaps from the *Kalmucks to Norway; and it is as well known in Japan as it was to the Brothers Grimm. The details vary from place to place, for the chivalric chase is variously aided by magical horses, telescopes, medical skill, military prowess, knowledge of everything in the world, or the power to run faster than thought. In Iceland, the girl is sick; in Arabia a magic carpet is called into play; in Grimm, a tailor is one of the heroes – his skill is such that he can even sew eggs together. In the version of the Tales of a Parrot, set in Afghanistan, a dispute about the girl arises between the heroes which may continue to this day; and in the Mongolian version the youths kill one another when they realise how beautiful the Princess is.*

In the Arabian telling, the lady's problem is that she is ill with a mysterious disease; in Germany and Japan, her captor is a dragon, in India, a demon, in the Mongolian, a wicked Khan has stolen her.

In the ancient Indian version, there is only one hero; in

one Persian variety and the Arabic, three; Grimm and another Persian recension have four brothers; the Kalmucks prefer six – and the Albanians opt for seven. The 47th tale of the Italian Basile's Pentamerone *is very close to the Arabic; yet the Italian version was known in Europe long before the modern translations of the* Arabian Nights *were published. This is the Albanian telling.*

ONCE UPON A time there was a King who had a beautiful daughter. They lived happily until, one day, the Devil took it into his head to carry her away. This he did, conveying her to his dwelling-place, deep in the earth, where human beings cannot normally reach.

The King was distraught beyond measure; and he announced that whoever should save the girl could have her hand in marriage, provided that she agreed to accept him.

Seven intelligent, noble and skilful youths each volunteered to rescue the Princess, and they set out together to seek the hiding-place.

Now these brothers were well equipped for their task. The first had such acute hearing that he could hear any sound, even from the most remote distances. The second had the power of making the very earth open to any depth. The third could steal anything from anyone without their knowing it. The fourth could hurl any object to the very confines of the world. The fifth was able to build a lofty and impregnable castle in an instant. The sixth was such a marksman that he could hit anything, no matter how high in the air it was, or how distant. The seventh could catch, and safely hold, anything which fell from the sky, whatever the altitude.

The seven had not gone very far when the youth with the acute hearing put his ear to the ground and heard that under that very spot was the Devil's hideout. He said to the second young man:

'Cause the earth to open at this point!'

Instantly, by the second youth's magical power, the earth opened; and the party descended into the ground to where they saw the Devil, deeply asleep and snoring, clutching the maiden to him.

The third youth stole the Princess from the diabolical grasp by his power to abstract anything from anywhere without it being known. In her place he put a toad.

The fourth companion took off one of the Devil's unique shoes, and hurled it so far that it descended at the other end of the earth.

Carrying the Princess, the brothers started their journey back to her father's palace.

Very soon, however, the Devil awoke. He roared and screamed with fury when he found the toad, the Princess gone and his irreplaceable shoe missing. He threw himself into the air and sped to the end of the world to recover the footgear, and then started off in hot pursuit of the travellers.

As soon as they saw him coming in the distance, the fifth young man caused by his art a mighty and almost inaccessible tower to be built. The eight fugitives went inside, and the door closed, just at the moment when the Devil arrived.

Try as he might, the fiend could not get into the tower. Resorting to guile, he said:

'I will go away in peace, if you will only just let me have one final look at the Princess.'

Foolishly, as it turned out, they made a very small hole in the tower for him to peep in: and in less time than it takes to tell, he had pulled the girl through this aperture, and was flying away with her through the air towards his foul abode.

Now the sixth young man, taking his magical bow, sped an arrow towards the Devil, hitting him so hard and true that he dropped the Princess, from an immense height.

The seventh youth was ready: and he caught her before she hit the ground.

Soon they reached the palace in safety, and the King was overjoyed at the return of his daughter. 'Which of the brothers will you choose?' he asked her.

'Each one of them has done something indispensable to rescue me,' said the Princess, 'yet I think that I will choose the one who caught me when I fell.'

This seventh youth was, as it happens, the youngest and the most handsome, so they were married. And the King rewarded all the other young men with lavish presents and grants of land, and they all lived happily ever afterwards.

The Algonquin Cinderella

At the end of the 19th century, Mrs M. R. Cox collected three hundred years of Cinderella-type stories. They totalled 345 versions: and she added that they could be multiplied. This may be one of the most enduring of all tales – a variety has been noted (by Arthur Waley) in a Chinese book of the ninth century AD. My father published a Vietnamese variant, claimed to be thousands of years old, in 1960. It has also been observed that the story of Aslaug, daughter of Siegfried and Brunhild in the Volsung Saga, is a striking parallel. Apart from the now-popular version of Perrault, published in the 18th century, there are other intriguing and excellent tales featuring the pathetic Cinders. Of these, the Scottish variant is 'Rashin Coatie' – Coat of Rushes – and there is an English one: 'Cap o' Rushes'. People have argued about the slipper – should it have been glass or fur. Children love the details of the ball, the magic pumpkin, the wicked stepmother, and why should they not? But for sheer beauty and delight, this American version, found among the Algonquin Indians, seems hard to beat.

THERE WAS ONCE a large village of the MicMac Indians of the Eastern Algonquins, built beside a lake. At the far end of the settlement stood a lodge, and in it lived a being who was always invisible. He had a sister who looked after him, and everyone knew that any girl who could see him might marry him. For that reason there were very few girls who did not try, but it was very long before anyone succeeded.

This is the way in which the test of sight was carried out: at evening-time, when the Invisible One was due to be returning home, his sister would walk with any girl who might come down to the lakeshore. She, of course, could see her brother, since he was always visible to her. As soon as she saw him, she would say to the girls:

'Do you see my brother?'

'Yes,' they would generally reply – though some of them did say 'No.'

To those who said that they could indeed see him, the sister would say:

'Of what is his shoulder strap made?'

Some people say that she would enquire:

'What is his moose-runner's haul?' or 'With what does he draw his sled?' And they would answer:

'A strip of rawhide' or 'a green flexible branch', or something of that kind.

Then she, knowing that they had not told the truth, would say:

'Very well, let us return to the wigwam!'

When they had gone in, she would tell them not to sit in a certain place, because it belonged to the Invisible One. Then, after they had helped to cook the supper, they would wait with great curiosity, to see him eat. They could be sure that he was a real person, for when he took off his moccasins they became visible, and his sister hung them up. But beyond this they saw nothing of him, not even when they stayed in the place all the night, as many of them did.

Now there lived in the village an old man who was a widower, and his three daughters. The youngest girl was very small, weak and often ill; and yet her sisters, especially the elder, treated her cruelly. The second daughter was kinder, and sometimes took her side, but the wicked sister would burn her hands and feet with hot cinders, and she was covered with scars from this treatment. She was so marked that people called her Oochigeaskw, the Rough-Faced Girl.

When her father came home and asked why she had such burns, the bad sister would at once say that it was her own fault, for she had disobeyed orders and gone near the fire and fallen into it.

These two elder sisters decided one day to try their luck at seeing the Invisible One. So they dressed themselves in their finest clothes, and tried to look their prettiest. They found the Invisible One's sister and took the usual walk by the water.

When he came, and when they were asked if they could see him, they answered: 'Of course.' And when asked about the shoulder strap or sled cord, they answered: 'A piece of rawhide.'

But of course they were lying like the others, and they got nothing for their pains.

The next afternoon, when the father returned home, he brought with him many of the pretty little shells from which wampum was made, and they set to work to string them.

That day, poor little Oochigeaskw, who had always gone barefoot, got a pair of her father's moccasins, old ones, and put them into water to soften them so that she could wear them. Then she begged her sisters for a few wampum shells. The elder called her a 'little pest', but the younger one gave her some. Now, with no other clothes than her usual rags, the poor little thing went into the woods and got herself some sheets of birch bark, from which she made a dress, and put marks on it for decoration, in the style of long ago. She made a petticoat and a loose gown, a cap, leggings and a handkerchief. She put on her father's large old moccasins, which were far too big for her, and went forth to try her luck. She would try, she thought, to discover whether she could see the Invisible One.

She did not begin very well. As she set off, her sisters shouted and hooted, hissed and yelled, and tried to make her stay. And the loafers around the village, seeing the strange little creature, called out 'Shame!'

The poor little girl in her strange clothes, with her face all scarred, was an awful sight, but she was kindly received by the sister of the Invisible One. And this was, of course, because this noble lady understood far more about things than simply the mere outside which all the rest of the world knows. As the brown of the evening sky turned to black, the lady took her down to the lake.

'Do you see him?' the Invisible One's sister asked.

'I do, indeed – and he is wonderful!' said Oochigeaskw.

The sister asked:

'And what is his sled-string?'

The little girl said:

'It is the Rainbow.'

'And, my sister, what is his bow-string?'

'It is The Spirit's Road – the Milky Way.'

'So you *have* seen him,' said his sister. She took the girl home with her and bathed her. As she did so, all the scars disappeared from her body. Her hair grew again, as it was combed, long, like a blackbird's wing. Her eyes were now like stars: in all the world there was no other such beauty. Then, from her treasures, the lady gave her a wedding garment, and adorned her.

Then she told Oochigeaskw to take the *wife's* seat

in the wigwam: the one next to where the Invisible One sat, beside the entrance. And when he came in, terrible and beautiful, he smiled and said:

'So we are found out!'

'Yes,' said his sister. And so Oochigeaskw became his wife.

FINIS